D0986686

American
Federalism: *A View
from the States*

American Federalism: *A View from the States*

DANIEL J. ELAZAR
Temple University

Thomas Y. Crowell Company NEW YORK
Established 1834

Theodore Lownik Library
Illinois Benedictine College
Lisle, Illinois 60532

JK
325
.E39

To Michael Albert

Copyright © 1966 by Thomas Y. Crowell Company

ALL RIGHTS RESERVED

No part of this book may be reproduced in any form, by mimeograph or any other means, without permission in writing from the publisher, except by a reviewer, who may quote brief passages in a review to be published in a magazine or newspaper.

LIBRARY OF CONGRESS CATALOG CARD NUMBER: 66-17590

Designed by Judith Woracek Barry

MANUFACTURED IN THE UNITED STATES OF AMERICA
BY VAIL-BALLOU PRESS, INC., BINGHAMTON, N. Y.

First Printing, June, 1966
Second Printing, October, 1966

PREFACE

In recent years, a number of very useful and important studies of American federalism have added substantially to our knowledge of the American political system and our understanding of the way that system, in all its parts, is animated by federal principles. These studies, while breaking new ground, have tended to view the system either from a national perspective, seeking an overview of the whole, or from the perspective of our local communities, especially the nation's metropolitan areas, seeking their role in a system of government still in process of adjusting to the demands of the metropolitan frontier. The states —traditionally the "men in the middle"—inevitably have been studied as parts of the federal system, but treated only rarely as the pivotal parts they are. Thus, a gap has been left in the corpus of materials available to students of federalism and American government.

This volume represents a modest effort to fill that gap, to examine American federalism from the perspective of the states. It is based on the best of the recent research into the problem, including the author's own work over the past decade. It is also intended to be a step toward expanding our knowledge of the states as political systems and some of the fundamental forces shaping them as civil societies.

This book is not meant to be comprehensive, but neither is it incomplete. I have tried to convey a sense of the states' place as participants in what I have elsewhere called "the American partnership," by emphasizing those factors that are most important in shaping their place. If there is any single point the book tries to make about the American political system as a whole it is that the system is—or, at its best, strives to be—a partnership, of governments and publics and individuals. Indeed, the federal principle, which I argue (in the following pages and elsewhere) is the animating principle of the American political process, calls intrinsically for partnership. The very term "federal" comes from the Latin word for covenant, indicating that federalism is best conceived as the end product of a compact or covenant uniting separate parties without merging them —in other words, a partnership. We need not go to Latin sources to gain this sense of the meaning of the American system. If, for some outlandish reason, Americans were ever to adopt an ideologically correct salutation to parallel that of the communists' "comrade," they would be very likely to select the classic greeting of the cowboy, the archetypal American folk figure, "pardner," which conveys just that sense of independent interdependence that characterizes American federalism.

It will be clear to the reader that I value the federal system and the states as equal partners in it. Any reforms I am likely to propose would be directed to improving the system as a partnership and to strengthening the place of the states as its keystones. While I value the system as it exists, it is also clear that one need not be a separatist to see the problems of overcentralization nor a collectivist to understand the problems of excessive localism. Both kinds of problems do exist, and if this volume does not explore them thoroughly enough, it is only because I have chosen to devote the available space to first understanding the partnership in its strengths, which, I would argue, far outweigh its weaknesses. The reader is better forewarned that this is so.

Certain segments of this book first appeared as parts of Chapter Twelve, "The States and the Nation," in Herbert Jacob and Kenneth N. Vines, eds., *Politics in the American States,* published by Little, Brown and Company, whose permission to use the material is gratefully acknowledged. Thanks are due the editors of that volume without whom it may truly be said that this book would never have been written. I am exceedingly grate-

Preface

ful to my friend and colleague, Harold Chase, who read the original manuscript and actively encouraged me to seek its publication. Most of my research into federal-state-local relations embodied in Chapter Seven was carried on under the auspices of the Institute of Government and Public Affairs of the University of Illinois. In many important ways, this book is really another product of the University of Chicago federalism workshop directed by my friend and teacher the late Morton Grodzins. Not only does it draw heavily on the research of the workshop members, particularly that of Kenneth E. Gray and E. Lester Levine, but many of its central hypotheses are extensions or modifications of those formulated in the workshop. My thanks are also due the John Simon Guggenheim Foundation whose generosity made it possible for me to devote the time necessary to complete this work. Herman Makler, of the editorial staff of the Thomas Y. Crowell Company College Department, performed all the functions an editor should in a manner that went beyond any author's expectations. Needless to say, the work itself is fully my own responsibility.

My wife Harriet has been of inestimable value, encouraging my efforts and then acting as both secretary and typist to bring them to fruition. In the last analysis, it was she who made it possible for this book to reach the presses in the course of a very busy year.

A good scholar writes a book to ask as well as answer important questions. I would like to think that among those who read this book there will be people who will be encouraged by this modest effort to seek and find better—or at least more comprehensive—answers than those suggested in the following pages.

D.J.E.

Golden Valley, Minn.

CONTENTS

[ix]

CHAPTER FOUR

The States and the Political Setting, 79

CHAPTER FIVE

Varying Responses to the Partnership, 117

Contents

CHAPTER SIX

Protecting the States' Integrity, 141

CHAPTER SEVEN

The States and Their Civil Communities, 163

CHAPTER ONE

Systems and Issues

The States as Systems within a System

The fifty American states, located between the powerful federal government and the burgeoning local governments in a metropolitanizing nation, are the keystones of the American governmental arch. This was the case when the Constitution was adopted in 1789 and remains true despite the great changes that have taken place in the intervening years.

This assertion runs counter to most contemporary perceptions of American government. If it were based upon an analysis of the present position of the states in light of formal *constitutional* interpretations alone, there would be great difficulty in substantiating it. In fact, the states maintain their central role because of their *political* position in the overall framework of the nation's political system, a position supported by the Constitution but which transcends its formal bounds. Unlike the more or less visible constitutional status of the states, their political position is generally of low visibility, not only to the public at large but often even to those people involved in the day-to-day operations of American government.

This volume is devoted to an exploration of the way in which the states function as political keystones, serving their local subdivisions and supporting the overall structure of national government. The central theme is twofold: (1) the states are, at one and the same time, well-integrated parts of the overall American civil society and also separate civil societies in their own right with their own political systems, and (2) the states have preserved their integrity not through a sharp separation of their political systems from the national system but within an intricate framework of cooperative relationships that preserve their structural integrity while tying all levels of government together functionally in the common task of serving the American people.[1]

Federalism can be defined as the mode of political organization that unites smaller polities within an overarching political system by distributing power among general and constituent governments in a manner designed to protect the existence and authority of both national and subnational political systems, enabling all to share in the overall system's decision-making and executing processes. In its simplest form, federalism means national unification through the maintenance of subnational systems. In its largest sense, however, federalism is more than an arrangement of governmental structures; it is a mode of political activity that requires certain kinds of cooperative relationships through the political system it animates. Federalism is the central characteristic of the American political system, its principles animating the greater part of the nation's political process. The idea of the federal union as a partnership is a key aspect of federalism. This idea of partnership has been extended far beyond the simple sense of a relationship between the federal and state governments to become the guiding

---

[1] The terms "state," "civil society," and "political system" are used in relation to one another throughout this chapter and should be understood clearly. *State* is used in the common manner in reference to the fifty politically delineated constituent entities that make up the United States.

Every state (as well as the United States as a whole) is a *civil society*, a relatively complex social system organized and defined politically which (1) pursues a particular conception of justice that it makes its own; (2) encompasses a wide variety of social and economic interests; (3) is charged with considerable responsibility for satisfying the technological, economic, and political needs of its people; and (4) is capable of authoritatively mobilizing the resources necessary to do so in a manner sufficient to ensure its own maintenance. Every state (and every nation) exists as a society because it is defined and delineated politically, or civilly, hence the term "civil society." Using less technical imagery, a civil society is one which, in commonsense terms, could stand alone as a sovereign nation. Obviously, the American states do not, but if by some quirk of fate it were to become necessary,

principle in most of the political relationships that tie institutions, groups, interests, and individuals together in the American political order, animating public-private relations as well as intergovernmental ones. The term itself has come into common usage. We all recognize the frequent references made to the "partnerships" between "government and business"; between "labor and management"; as well as to those between governments.

Partnership implies the distribution of real power among several centers which must negotiate cooperative arrangements with one another in order to achieve common goals. This arrangement is often mislabeled decentralization but more appropriately could be called noncentralization. The American federal union differs from a decentralized political system in that constitutional limits are imposed on the extent to which the national government can concentrate as well as devolve governmental power and functions. At the same time, the union obviously differs from a confederation of essentially separate political systems where the center is continually weak. In the noncentralized American system, there is no central government with absolute authority over the states in the unitary sense, but a strong national government cou-

most of them could carry out the functions of full sovereignty with little adjustment of their political institutions and any of them could do so at least as well as the bulk of the new "sovereign" nations of the post-World War II era.

Every state, as a civil society, possesses its own *political system* to handle its internal government and authoritatively manage the pursuit of common political ends. This political system, which includes the formal agencies of government and the structure of internal interest and electoral groups that influence the formulation and execution of public policy within the boundaries of the state, is one of a number of "systems" (i.e., the social system, the educational system) that together make up a civil society. For a discussion of the philosophic roots of the concept of civil society, see Leo Strauss, *Natural Right and History* (Chicago: University of Chicago Press, 1953), pp. 130–132. For an elaboration of the conception of the political system used here, see David Easton, *The Political System* (New York: Knopf, 1953), Chapter 5. For a discussion of what constitutes a society in the first place, see Talcott Parsons, "Society," in *Encyclopedia of the Social Sciences* (New York: Macmillan, 1931).

pled with strong state governments in which authority and power are shared, constitutionally and practically.[2]

What deserves careful attention is the fact that the American federal system is both a single system and a system of systems at the same time. This permanent feature of American government was defined very precisely by Chief Justice Salmon P. Chase just after the Civil War.

The perpetuity and indissolubility of the Union, by no means implies the loss of distinct and individual existence . . . of . . . the States . . . "Without the States in union, there could be no such political body as the United States" . . . The preservation of the States, and the maintenance of their governments, are as much within the design and care of the Constitution as the preservation of the Union and the maintenance of the National government. The Constitution, in all of its provisions, looks to an indestructible Union, composed of indestructible States.[3]

Bearing in mind the essential sameness of the idea that the states are systems within a larger system and the idea that the United States is "an indestructible Union, composed of indestructible States," it is possible to examine the politics of American federalism with understanding.

Federalism and Political Issues

In the United States, the very existence of federalism requires that virtually all political issues be considered with two questions in mind: *What kinds of issues are raised in American politics because the states (and their cities) exist as they do?* and *How are*

[2] The very word *decentralization* implies the legal investment of power in a central government which may choose to devolve powers on local governments or not, as it wills. The desires and interests of the local governments can be made effective only insofar as they can be effectively expressed by local representatives in the councils of the central government. In any decentralized system, the ultimate power—including the power to alter or abolish all subnational governments—rests with the central government. For further discussion of these distinctions, see the articles on "Decentralization," "Federalism," and "Federation" in *Encyclopedia of the Social Sciences* (New York: Macmillan, 1931).

[3] *Texas* v. *White*, 7 Wallace 700 (1869).

issues developed and resolved in the American political system because of the existence of the states (and their cities) in their present form?

The relevance of these questions is nowhere more apparent than in the civil rights issues that face the "white" nations of the world today. Aside from the basic moral considerations raised by the question of equal rights for nonwhites and other minority groups, different political systems face the issue quite differently. In the United Kingdom, the Negro question is most frequently discussed in terms of Commonwealth relations externally and class attitudes internally. In the U.S.S.R., the essential question (insofar as it is discussed) may well revolve around the effects of discrimination on the Soviet effort to win the Afro-Asian nations to communism. In South Africa the central question is the sheer existence of a white minority on a black continent without serious regard for problems of constitutionalism on either side. In the new nations of black Africa, on the other hand, the issue is perceived as one of emancipation from the bonds of colonialism and achievement of status equal to that of the whites.

In the United States, the immediate problems of overcoming racial discrimination are inevitably linked to the enduring problems of federalism. No consideration of these problems as political issues can escape questions of federal jurisdiction, states' rights, the role of the United States Supreme Court as an arbiter of federal-state relations, constitutional guarantees of internal autonomy to the states, and the constitutionally guaranteed power of the states and localities in national politics. Federal intervention to help overcome discrimination is managed on a state by state basis and progress is measured the same way.

Some say that when we talk about the states in the federal system we are talking about a "mere" *structural* question; the Negro rights issue reveals just how *political* this structural question is. Despite constant reaffirmations by the federal courts in the past two decades that Negro rights are protected under the United States Constitution, and despite presidential willingness to intervene with force where the states allow these rights to be publicly suppressed by force, the entire question of Negro rights remains greatly dependent on the willingness of the states to aid in carrying out, or in complying with, national policy. This remains true even in the face of the civil rights legislation enacted in 1964 and 1965 which legally clarifies national policy and provides the means for enforcement of national constitutional provisions guaranteeing equal rights.

Moreover, the differing responses of the several states to this issue make it clear that the bundle of individual characteristics combined to make up the political entity we call a "state" adds up to something more than a territory marked off by lines on the map of the continent. In Chief Justice Chase's words again:

[The word *state*] describes sometimes a people or community of individuals united more or less closely in political relations, inhabiting temporarily or permanently the same country; often it denotes only the country or territorial region, inhabited by such a community; not infrequently it is applied to the government under which the people live; . . . In the Constitution the term state most frequently expresses the combined idea . . . of people, territory, and government.[4]

If the usage of the term "people" is understood to mean the particular complex of human culture by which human beings individually and collectively invest particular communities with character, then it becomes very likely, if not inevitable, that each state will possess its own particular characteristics simply by virtue of its settled existence over generations. In turn, its bundle of individual characteristics is what transforms each state into a civil society, possessing a political system that is in some measure autonomous. And despite the apparently great and continuing pressures for centralization, this autonomy is no mean thing.

The Negro rights problem, in many respects, represents the hardest possible case for demonstrating the noncentralizing influence of federalism and the role of the states as civil societies. Here is a problem in which the moral issue is paramount. Even if the Constitution did not offer the guarantees it does, there would be great pressure on the federal government and the states to secure full rights of citizenship for Negroes. Furthermore, here is

⁴ *Ibid.*

a problem of majority-minority relations among the states themselves: fewer than one-fifth of the states are resisting national demands on this issue, while most of the remaining four-fifths are actively committed as states to national policies in regard to Negro rights.

With explicit constitutional guarantees of one hundred years' standing *plus* a generation of court rulings *plus* federal executive and legislative actions in the past decade to enforce those guarantees *plus* the legislative and executive action of some thirty-five states to extend civil rights beyond existing federal law, one might expect the minority of more or less recalcitrant states of the South to succumb, willingly or not, to the overwhelming influence and power of the nation as a whole. Indeed, if southern resistance were only a matter of localities directly opposing the concentrated might of a central government, overt resistance would undoubtedly have been overcome some time ago, simply through the subordination of the local governments to an overwhelmingly powerful political system.

The existence of a federal system functioning in the American manner changes not only the terms of the issue but the manner of its resolution. For under the American federal system as it is presently constituted, the actual implementation of the relevant constitutional doctrines, be they "separate but equal" or "equal and not separate," lies primarily with the states. Although the national constitution may set the standard and the Supreme Court the guidelines, the state governments are left to apply those guidelines within their own boundaries in a manner consonant with their respective political cultures. Only in those cases where it has been clearly demonstrated that the states cannot or will not implement the Constitution as interpreted does it become possible for the federal authorities to intervene. With some exceptions, even the right of intervention was not authorized until passage of the civil rights legislation of 1964 and 1965. Furthermore, this power to intervene, which has been viewed as a great extension of the federal role, is extremely limited, and in no case can intervention be more than temporary.

Even when the federal government has the authority to act,

it tends to use great self-restraint in the exercise of its authority. It must do so to preserve the federal system simply because it possesses overwhelming power. President Kennedy demonstrated this use of self-restraint in the University of Mississippi integration crisis of 1962. Constitutionally, he could have ordered the U.S. Army to occupy the university campus in Oxford, Mississippi, and secure the peace once trouble had begun in the area. He apparently recognized, however, that the immediate use of troops would have raised other problems in terms of the public reaction to an apparent federal encroachment upon traditional state peace-keeping functions. Consequently, he initially refrained from taking such a drastic step, sending U.S. marshals to enforce the orders of the federal courts instead. Only after the marshals were placed under siege did he resort to the stronger weapon, military occupation, and even then he clearly indicated the limited nature of his action. At that point, he had strong public sentiment on his side.

School integration, the first target of recent efforts to desegregate the southern states, is a particularly revealing case. Though federal efforts led to some school desegregation in all the segregated states except Mississippi, by 1964, ten years after the Supreme Court's desegregation decision, only 9 per cent of the school children in the border states and less than 1 per cent in the states of Deep South were in integrated schools.

Table 1 shows that there is no easy correlation between the extent of federal pressure and the degree of school desegregation achieved in any particular state. The best correlation is an inverse one: the more open pressure, the less desegregation. This is not a cause and effect relationship but is symptomatic of the power of the states to maintain previously established positions even in the face of federal power. It is clear that desegregation has gone further in those states whose leadership decided to comply with the Supreme Court ruling without additional federal pressure. This has been confirmed by a number of case studies of desegregation in the border states. Those states that have chosen nominal compliance have generally been able to maintain their own "time-

Table 1. Federal Pressure and School Desegregation in Southern States (Percentage of Total Number of Negro School Children Attending Desegregated Schools)

STATE	JUNE, 1963	DECEMBER, 1963	MAY, 1964

1. States complying with Supreme Court rulings with state and local public support. Federal pressure confined to occasional court rulings.

Delaware	55.9	55.4	56.5
Kentucky	54.1	54.8	54.4
Maryland	45.1	48.3	47.8
Missouri	38.8	42.1	42.1
Oklahoma	23.6	28.1	28.0
West Virginia	61.4	87.9	58.2

2. States reluctantly complying with federal court rulings as issued to avoid showdown. Federal pressure confined to regular court rulings and low level or spot Justice Department intervention, usually in cooperation with state authorities.

Florida	.67	1.53	1.53
Georgia	.01	.05	.05
North Carolina [a]	.26	.54	.54
South Carolina	.00	.004	.004
Tennessee [a]	1.10	2.71	2.72
Texas [a]	2.30	4.29	5.52

3. States attempting massive resistance but abandoning tactic for reluctant compliance. Federal pressure has involved use of troops or marshals or heavy legal pressure.

Arkansas [b]	.21	.97	.33
Louisiana [b]	.04	.60	.60
Virginia	.53	1.57	1.63

4. States resisting desegregation massively through agencies of state and local government. Federal pressure involves regular use of troops and/or U.S. marshals.

Alabama	.000	.004	.007
Mississippi	.000	.000	.000

[a] Violent local resistance to state's decision to comply reduced by state intervention.

[b] State compliance modified by state-sanctioned local resistance.

SOURCE: *Southern School News*, June 1964.

tables," slow as they may be. Furthermore, regardless of the kind of federal pressure applied for the past ten years, state governments in the Deep South have been able to continue segregation practices in nearly pristine form, often restoring segregated conditions after the federal intervention has spent itself or, in any case, confining integration to a token level.

In the fall of 1965, the slow pace of the first ten years was considerably accelerated as a result of the 1964 Civil Rights Act, which, among other things, provides that federal funds can be withheld from school districts refusing to desegregate. Though the amount of money involved for most southern school districts is not great, by September 1965 over 90 per cent of the school districts in the Southern States had indicated their willingness to comply with the new legislation—at least on paper. Even so, the percentage of the total number of Negro school children attending desegregated schools actually increased from 2.5 to only about 5 per cent.

No doubt many school districts filing compliance plans with the United States Office of Education did so in the hope of taking the pressure of the law off them. Those districts will very likely try to maintain fully or substantially segregated schools through their continuing power to administer their own systems as agents of their states under the United States Constitution. This, too, is an aspect of their opportunity in the federal system. Nevertheless, school desegregation appears bound to diminish, not only because of pressures from federal agencies, but also because the norms of local school desegregation are no longer simply matters of national policy with widespread support in the North and West. As time goes on, they are gaining support in the resisting states as well, not only among Negro citizens, but also from an increasing number of white citizens, who choose compliance in the name of law and order as a means to extricate themselves from a tradition that demands white conformance to a segregationist code.

In the end, the Negro victory will not be simply a consequence of superior federal strength in a contest with a number of recalcitrant states. It will mark a major change in the attitudes of the dominant groups in those states stimulated by the contest, a change created by the awakening of southern whites to the injustices of segregation in terms of American values which they share. It must be so because, when the present excitement has died down, as it will, the nature of American federalism is such that once a new consensus is achieved, these matters will again be fully entrusted to the local populations.

The States as Civil Societies

When we speak of a state's doing this or that or taking one position or another and of states' responding to federal actions in different ways, we are, like Chief Justice Chase, using a convenient way of speaking about the actions of those people and interests within each state's civil society that dominate its political system. This does not mean that the dominant forces leading a state represent all or even a majority of the citizens of their state every time they act in its name. Cross-pressures of varying degrees exist within each state on every issue. On most issues that attract nationwide attention, the cross-pressures extend across state lines. This means that contesting groups within the state's civil society may momentarily find they have more in common with their counterparts in other states than with their immediate compatriots. But there exists a wide range of issues in which the dominant interests in any state can act *as if* they had statewide consensus behind them. These include some substantive issues in which the welfare or interests of the bulk of a state's citizenry are clearly involved (such as state economic development) and certain fundamental procedural issues which are important because they concern the maintenance of the state itself (such as the right of the state to determine who can vote in its elections).

Proper use of the systemic aspects of a state's civil society enhances the possibility for the people and interests dominating the state's political system to speak in the name of their state. There is a wide variety of ways in which each state, as a reasonably autonomous civil society, can capitalize on its internal unity in the face of outside pressure. States can take appropriate legislative and executive action. (Virginians are able to prevent school desegregation by creating state-sanctioned private schools alongside the public schools, the former enjoying the wholehearted support of white families.) Local officials can enforce regulations and ordinances that, taken at face value, seem irrelevant to the issue at hand but can be applied discreetly in a relevant way. (Alabama city fathers are able to close a school integrated by federal order on grounds that it is a fire hazard.) Private exercise of property and personal rights backed by state and local law enforcement agencies can be used as a countervailing power. (Mississippi state and local officials are helped in their efforts to prevent Negroes from registering to vote by the eagerness of local newspapers to publish the names of those who try to register and by the active reprisals taken against them by private parties in a host of private actions.) Federal authorities, including the courts, have implicitly recognized that states do function as civil societies in this way by stamping as equally unconstitutional both direct state action and private actions sanctioned by the states and serving to reenforce racial segregation.[5]

The states' formal constitutional position, taken alone, would hardly be an adequate line of defense in cases where they have a paramount interest in preserving local patterns or customs, just as (to take a far different example) the states have no constitutional guarantee that their citizens will receive a specific share of federal defense expenditures. Even the states' role at the center of the nation's party system (see below) would not provide sufficient defense against concentrated national pressure, though it helps considerably. The states' first line of defense (or, in the case of defense contracts, offense) lies in their ability to function as civil societies, to mobilize many facets of their internal and external powers through their own political systems to resist "encroachments" (or to gain benefits) from the outside. In the militant states of the South, the state police, the local school

_____

[5] For some examples of state action of this sort before the turn of the century, see Gilbert T. Stephenson, *Race Distinctions in American Law* (New York: Appleton, 1910). For a history of such state actions and the federal reactions to them, see Albert T. Blaustein and Clarence C. Ferguson, *Desegregation and the Law* (New York: Vintage Books, 1963).

boards, the senators in Washington, the governor, the local fire inspectors, the network of Citizens Councils, all join together to fight desegregation. In every state, relevant groups of similar diversity—the state's economic development agency, state and local chambers of commerce, the governor and the mayors, and the state's representatives in Congress—join to secure defense contracts, federal installations, or public works. It is their ability to join together and to fight their common battle on a number of fronts that has given certain states such a large measure of success in these various endeavors.

Take a different kind of case involving defense against "outside encroachment." Where the state law enforcement agencies seek to resist certain Supreme Court rulings on criminal procedures, they are often able to do so if they can bring courts, prosecutors, police, and the bar together at the state level and in the state's communities in common agreement as to how the individual's basic rights are to be protected under the state's scheme and what law enforcement agencies are to be allowed to do so.[6]

While the extent to which a state possesses internal unity of purpose varies from issue to issue, there are some guidelines by which to assess the probable degree of internal unity. These include:

A. The degree of overall state deviation from national patterns and norms.

B. The degree of intrastate sharing of common patterns and norms.

C. The degree of overall state deviation from national policies and interests.

D. The degree of intrastate sharing of common policies and interests.

The interaction of these four factors is simply portrayed in Figure 1. The more all four factors are intensified (i.e., converge in the

[6] For a discussion of state actions to modify U. S. Supreme Court rulings, see Walter F. Murphy, "Lower Court Checks on Supreme Court Power," *American Political Science Review*, LIII, 4 (December, 1959), 1017–1031, and Glendon A. Schubert, *Constitutional Politics* (New York: Holt, Rinehart and Winston, 1960), pp. 259–263.

middle of the figure), the greater the likelihood of intrastate unity vis-à-vis the outside world, and vice versa. As an operational rule, it is generally reasonable to assume that the more frequently there is intrastate unity on specific issues, the greater is the likelihood for continued unity in the future.

Though little is known about the existence or character of internal unity in the individual states, it is possible to trace some overall patterns of internal unity or cohesiveness from the limited

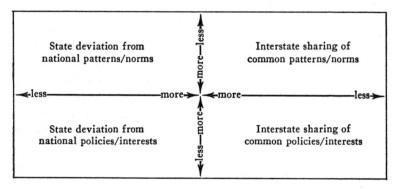

FIGURE 1. Factors Influencing the Degree of Internal Unity in the States

data at hand, provided the limits of both data and findings are recognized. A tentative state by state analysis, based on judicious consideration of the available evidence, is offered in Table 2 as a preliminary guide for the assessment of intrastate cohesiveness since 1945 in matters that transcend state boundaries to become national in concern.[7]

[7] Tabular presentation of this analysis is offered with some hesitancy because of the tendency to "harden" the meaning of tabular data, which, in this case, would be to go beyond the writer's very conservative intentions. The table represents the writer's own conclusions to date, based on his research over the past several years. In studying the problem of state unity against outside demands, he has explored the following sources of data: published studies directed toward other ends but bearing on these questions; state histories discussing relevant situations and controversies; public pronouncements of state officials on relevant issues; newspapers in leading cities

Detailed analysis of this table and commentary on the nuances of meaning that must be accounted for in explanation of the oversimplified summary it represents would require more space than is available here. By adding the numerical values of each of the four factors listed in the table, it is possible to establish a crude measure of internal unity for each state which can be used to compare internal unity state by state. The highest possible internal unity is represented by the lowest possible numerical total (4), while the lowest possible internal unity is represented by the highest possible total (12). The national order of state cohesiveness is shown in Table 3. States with four or five points are highly unified in both norms and policies and also tend to differ most from national patterns. States with six or seven points are highly unified in both categories but tend to follow national trends more closely. States with eight or nine points have much internal unity to fall back on when an issue of vital importance to the whole state arises but infrequently display unified reactions on national issues. States with ten or eleven points have highly divergent internal patterns and rarely unite over particular issues unless overall national unity is displayed.[8]

---

in the forty-eight mainland states (reviewed periodically at two- to five-year intervals since 1954); state by state and intrastate voting data in selected states for selected elections; and field work or disciplined observation in the forty-eight mainland states (at least two trips to each one). Published materials that bear directly on this issue are few. The reader is referred to the standard works on state politics of more recent vintage listed elsewhere in this volume and, more particularly, to the pioneering work of V. O. Key, Jr., *American State Politics: An Introduction* (New York: Knopf, 1956) and the highly perceptive if less scholarly work of John Gunther, *Inside USA* (New York: Harper, 1951). A good, if highly unorganized, source of data useful in developing general impressions of the state by state patterns is the collection of reports on federal-state-local relations of the House Intergovernmental Relations Subcommittee (Fountain Committee), 85th Congress, 1957 and 1958.

[8] It should be emphasized that the existence of a low level of intrastate cohesiveness does not necessarily mean that the citizens of a particular state do not identify strongly with their state. Very little is known about this particular question of state loyalties. What is clear is that such loyalties do exist, not in contradistinction to national loyalties, but as functions of the same patriotic sentiments that produce national loyalty.

Table 2. *Measures of the States' Internal Unity since 1945*

STATE (with unity index)	A	B	C	D	NORM OR ISSUE INVOLVING GREATEST INTERNAL UNITY VIS-À-VIS FEDERAL/OTHER GOVERNMENTS
Alabama (4)	1	1	1	1	Negro Rights [a]
Alaska (7)	2	1	2	2	Economic Development
Arizona (6)	2	1	2	1	Water Resources
Arkansas (4)	1	1	1	1	Negro Rights [a] and Economic Development
California (8)	2	1	3	2	Water Resources [b]
Colorado (7)	2	1	2	2	Water Resources [b]
Connecticut (10)	3	2	3	2	Metropolitan Problems
Delaware (10)	3	2	3	2	Maintenance of State's Economic Position
Florida (8)	1	3	1	3	Economic Development and Negro Rights [a]
Georgia (6)	1	2	1	2	Negro Rights [a]
Hawaii (8)	2	1	3	2	Communications with Mainland
Idaho (8)	2	2	2	2	Water Resources
Illinois (11)	3	3	2	3	Maintenance of State's Political Patterns
Indiana (8)	2	2	2	2	Maintenance of State's Political Patterns
Iowa (7)	2	1	2	2	Agricultural Problems
Kansas (7)	2	1	2	2	Agricultural Problems
Kentucky (7)	1	2	2	2	Maintenance of State's Political Patterns
Louisiana (4)	1	1	1	1	Negro Rights [a]
Maine (6)	1	1	2	2	Maintenance of State's Cultural Patterns
Maryland (9)	2	2	3	2	Maintenance of State's Political Patterns
Massachusetts (10)	3	3	3	1	Economic Development
Michigan (11)	2	3	3	3	Economic Development
Minnesota (6)	1	1	3	1	Maintenance of State's Cultural Patterns
Mississippi (4)	1	1	1	1	Negro Rights [a]
Missouri (8)	2	2	2	2	Maintenance of State's Political Patterns
Montana (6)	2	1	2	1	Water Resources
Nebraska (7)	2	2	1	2	Agricultural Problems
Nevada (4)	1	1	1	1	Gambling
New Hampshire (8)	2	2	2	2	Maintenance of State's Cultural Patterns

STATE (with unity index)	A	B	C	D	NORM OR ISSUE INVOLVING GREATEST INTERNAL UNITY VIS-À-VIS FEDERAL/OTHER GOVERNMENTS
New Jersey (8)	3	1	3	1	Metropolitan Problems
New Mexico (7)	1	2	2	2	Economic Development
New York (11)	2	3	3	3	Economic Development
North Carolina (5)	1	1	2	1	Negro Rights [a] and Economic Development
North Dakota (6)	1	1	2	2	Agricultural Problems
Ohio (8)	2	2	2	2	Maintenance of State's Cultural Patterns
Oklahoma (5)	1	1	2	1	Water Resources
Oregon (6)	1	1	2	2	Maintenance of State's Cultural Patterns
Pennsylvania (9)	3	1	3	2	Economic Development
Rhode Island (8)	3	1	3	1	Metropolitan Problems
South Carolina (4)	1	1	1	1	Negro Rights [a]
South Dakota (7)	2	1	2	2	Agricultural Problems
Tennessee (5)	1	1	1	2	Negro Rights [a] and TVA
Texas (5)	1	1	1	2	Maintenance of State's Cultural Patterns
Utah (5)	1	1	2	1	Maintenance of State's Cultural Patterns
Vermont (5)	1	1	2	1	Maintenance of State's Cultural Patterns
Virginia (5)	1	1	2	1	Negro Rights [a] and Maintenance of State's Cultural Patterns
Washington (6)	2	1	2	1	Water Resources
West Virginia (5)	1	1	2	1	Economic Development
Wisconsin (7)	2	1	2	2	Economic Development
Wyoming (5)	1	1	2	1	Economic Development

KEY: A: Degree of overall state deviation from national patterns or norms.
B: Degree of intrastate sharing of common patterns or norms.
C: Degree of overall state deviation from national policies or interests.
D: Degree of intrastate sharing of common policies or interests.
1. Great deviation (A, C) or great sharing (B, D).
2. Moderate deviation (A, C) or moderate sharing (B, D).
3. Little deviation (A, C) or little sharing (B, D).

[a] Considering only the enfranchised white community which effectively speaks for the state.

[b] Unity vis-à-vis other states. Also involves the greatest internal conflict within the state.

Table 3. National Order of State Cohesiveness

4	5	6	7
Alabama	North Carolina	Arizona	Alaska
Arkansas	Oklahoma	Georgia	Colorado
Louisiana	Tennessee	Maine	Iowa
Mississippi	Texas	Minnesota	Kansas
Nevada	Utah	Montana	Kentucky
South Carolina	Vermont	North Dakota	Nebraska
	Virginia	Oregon	New Mexico
	West Virginia	Washington	South Dakota
	Wyoming		Wisconsin

8	9	10	11
California	Maryland	Connecticut	Illinois
Florida	Pennsylvania	Delaware	Michigan
Hawaii		Massachusetts	New York
Idaho			
Indiana			
Missouri			
New Hampshire			
New Jersey			
Ohio			
Rhode Island			

The southern states as a group rank highest in degree of intrastate unity and in degree of deviation from national patterns and policies. This is reflected in the frequency with which they come into conflict with the federal government speaking for the nation as a whole (not only in regard to Negro rights but also in such fields as criminal law and social welfare, to mention but two others) and in the high degree of intrastate cohesiveness they display in responding to outside pressure. Though most of them are presently taking their stand on the race issue, what their white majorities are in fact concerned with is the maintenance of particular cultural patterns which are substantially different from those of the rest of the country. This is the basis for their cohesiveness. In Texas and Virginia, where those cultural patterns are particularly unique and are well perceived locally, the larger question already outweighs the immediate issue of race.

The states of the Northwest (particularly Minnesota) appear to have a high degree of intrastate cohesiveness coupled with substantial deviation from certain overall national patterns and norms which is rarely visible because the specific policies and interests they favor are those favored by the nation as a whole. The larger industrial states of the Northeast have low levels of internal cohesiveness but also appear to have low levels of deviation from national patterns and interests. Thus the policies and programs endorsed by the dominant forces in those states coincide most frequently with those espoused in Washington. The southwestern states tend to be reasonably cohesive, and although none is closely connected to national patterns and interests, only one is as deviant as the majority of the southern states.

Variations from this sectional pattern can be explained by the specific patterns of the variant states. Thus the states of northern New England remain culturally more homogeneous than, as well as economically different from, their sisters in the Northeast and also remain more internally united and more sharply differentiated from the national pattern for that reason. The largest states in the area north of the Ohio River and east of the Mississippi tend to be less united internally than the smaller ones, primarily because their very size has allowed more cultural and economic diversity to develop within their boundaries, even with the same social and economic forces.

Turning to the last column of Table 2, it is apparent that the highest degree of internal unity in relation to a specific norm or issue is invariably connected with some issue that would be of central importance to any society. Maintenance of cultural norms is one such issue. Thus (considering only the enfranchised white community which has been overwhelmingly dominant), ten of the southern states are most united in regard to the Negro rights question. The high degree of internal cohesion and uniqueness characteristic of those states is undoubtedly connected with the fact that the major problem uniting their people concerns both a basic cultural pattern and an immediate political issue.[9] As the

---

[9] See V. O. Key, Jr., *Southern Politics* (New York: Knopf, 1949).

Negroes in those states acquire political power in their own right, the shape of both intra- and interstate relations in the South is likely to change drastically.

At the same time, seven states (aside from Texas and Virginia), all located outside the mainstream of American life in one way or another, have as their prime unifying interest a concern with maintaining certain distinctive cultural patterns which have been theirs throughout their history. Three of these are the states of northern New England which sit at the edge of the great northeastern megalopolis and are also the last preserves of the original Yankeedom. Ohio seeks to preserve a kind of rural life style on the borders of the nation's great urban belt. Minnesota and Oregon are northwestern states, originally settled by Yankees and Scandinavians, which developed certain patterns of culture sufficiently different from those of the rest of their respective regions to demand special consideration if they are to be preserved. Utah is in much the same position, intensified by its place as the world center of Mormonism.[10]

Economic issues make up a second category of vital concerns that unite the states internally.[11] Nine states (twelve if the three southern states that consider this problem of equal importance with the race question are included) are most united in matters of economic development. Six of them are concentrated in the greater Northeast. In some cases (Massachusetts and New York,

[10] This is a difficult interest to describe with precision and, indeed, varies from state to state in its practical meaning. In Minnesota, it tends to be a generally felt consensus that the state is more "honest," more "community-minded," more "stable," more "homey," and more concerned with the individual than are the centers of the nation, and more "vital" and "progressive" than its immediate neighbors; that all this is due to the state's more isolated position; and that it is worth preserving. Some of these attitudes show up periodically in the Minneapolis *Tribune*'s "Minnesota Poll." In Texas, on the other hand, "preservation of cultural patterns" manifests itself concretely in wide circles as antifederal, antisocial welfare, antitax radicalism tied in with very clear economic interests in the state. See, for example, John Bainbridge, *The Super-Americans* (New York: Doubleday, 1961). See also Frank Jonas, ed., *Western Politics* (Salt Lake City: University of Utah Press, 1961).

[11] See Donald Gilmore, *Developing the "Little Economics"* (Committee on Economic Development, 1960).

for example), economic development is an issue which calls forth a unified public response despite an overall lack of state unity. In other cases (such as Michigan), even economic development is relatively weak as a unifying force, although it represents the only area in which substantial unity exists and the base upon which those interested in promoting intrastate cohesiveness are trying to build. In the Appalachian states suffering from major regional depressions, such as Pennsylvania and West Virginia, it is the most vital issue of all, while in North Carolina and Florida it has become important enough to divert public attention from exclusive focus on the race issue. Several other states are equally interested in other aspects of economic concern, such as Delaware's concern with maintenance of its economic position as the nominal headquarters of the nation's great corporations.

Larger socio-economic issues affecting whole civil societies predominate in the smaller of more homogeneous states. In three of the smaller northeastern states (Connecticut, New Jersey, and Rhode Island) where urbanization has passed the 80 per cent mark and is spread more or less evenly throughout each state, the problems of metropolitanization are central.[12] By the same token, five of the Plains states (Iowa, Kansas, Nebraska, and the Dakotas) are most united on agricultural matters.[13]

Seven of the western states, all except one moderately cohesive and nationally distinctive, stand most united over the issue of water resource development, a matter crucial for the sheer survival of their people. It should be noted in this connection that the very issue which unites two of these states vis-à-vis the rest of the nation also divides them most sharply in their internal politics. Thus northern and southern California stand together to resist the demands of Arizona and the other Colorado River states and then fight over the internal distribution of the waters they win.[14]

[12] See Jean Gottmann, *Megalopolis: The Urbanized Eastern Seaboard of the United States* (New York: Twentieth Century Fund, 1961).

[13] See Carl F. Kraenzel, *The Great Plains in Transition* (Norman: University of Oklahoma Press, 1959).

[14] See Dean E. Mann, *The Politics of Water in Arizona* (Tucson: University of Arizona Press, 1963).

Five states, all located along the middle of the country between North and South and all ranking low in internal cohesiveness, are united primarily in their concern with maintenance of the established political patterns which give them power against various pressures, usually external. Since there is little that unites the public in these states, the problems of the powerholders remain the most significant ones. They include the maintenance of low tax rates against the pressures of rising needs for governmental services, the maintenance of patronage systems in the face of pressures for civil service reform, and the maintenance of entrenched political organizations and alignments against disturbing elements that are generated from outside the state boundaries.[15]

The existence of one or two particularly important issues that perennially serve to unite each state internally should not obscure the existence of other issues which serve the same unifying purposes from time to time. Economic development issues, for example, are important unifying forces in every state. So, too, are issues involving the maintenance of the vested political interests in each state. And no state is without certain cultural patterns that the bulk of its articulate public considers unique and worth preserving.

The particular issues that unite the states internally are all deeply rooted in their respective geographic and historical settings. This is natural enough since each state acquires the common traditions, needs, and interests that give it meaning as a civil society through its particular combination of unique geographical and historical patterns, even when the meaning of these patterns is not readily understood by the state's citizenry. It seems obvious to say that every state has its own geography and history, but considering the American penchant for focusing on national patterns without considering subnational differences, even the obvious must sometimes be reaffirmed.

[15] See, among other sources, John H. Fenton, *Politics in the Border States* (New Orleans: The Hauser Press, 1957).

Federalism and Nationwide Political Concerns

The desegregation issue represents one of the many areas of political concern or conflict that influence and are influenced by the state-federal relationship. It is actually but one facet of the nationwide concern with civil rights that is currently attracting the attention of citizens of every stripe and governments at every level all over the United States. In this case, shared political concern means a measure of intergovernmental conflict because, in certain states, divergent interests are aligned with different levels of government. In other cases where the alignments of interests do not coincide with the structural divisions of federalism, shared concern is more likely to mean conflict that cuts across the state-federal division and, ultimately, state-federal collaboration in its resolution or in the development of substantive programs to cope with the area of concern as a whole.

There is abundant evidence that, since the earliest days of independence, when a problem has emerged as a public concern in the United States, it has emerged as a concern of publics at all levels of government, in the states and localities as well as in the nation as a whole, without regard for niceties of structure.[16] The list of nationwide concerns at any given point in time is bound to be a long one, and different concerns are likely to attract the attention and interest of different kinds of publics to differing degrees.

It is possible to chart the scope of any of those concerns and to treat its impact on state-federal political relations generally, in regard to groups of states and in regard to individual states, by considering (1) the essential character of the problems raised by each concern; (2) the essential distribution of authority and power between the federal government and the states; (3) the essential operational relationships between the two; (4) the es-

---

[16] The author has described this phenomenon in some detail in Daniel J. Elazar, *The American Partnership* (Chicago: University of Chicago Press, 1962), Part Three.

sential subareas or subconflicts within each area, where any exist; (5) the essential position of the states as states, if the individual states take any position, in regard to the concern or any of its subareas; (6) the important interests aligned on various sides; and (7) any special considerations that should be weighed when viewing the specific issues involved. By considering each of these seven points, we can develop a framework for analyzing any issue affecting state-federal relations.

The issue of desegregation, for example, is essentially a problem of implementing generally accepted principles of social and political equality for American citizens born Negro. Although the problem is considered primarily in relation to the South, where these principles are not generally accepted as applying to Negroes, it is also a problem in the rest of the nation, where there are great gaps between principle and practice. Since the Civil War era, authority for dealing with this problem has been shared by the federal government and the states, by formal constitutional grant. Until recently the bulk of the power to deal with the problem (as distinct from the authority to exercise power) was left in the hands of the states, but since the late 1940's, the federal share of that power has been growing. The 1964 Civil Rights Act represents, in certain respects, a "treaty" between the states and the federal government providing for a formal reallocation of that power, by which the representatives of the states "in Congress assembled" have consented to federal use of this power to backstop the efforts of those states willing to exercise power to maintain the rights of racial minorities and to force the citizens of states unwilling to do so to comply with national constitutional standards.

The 1964 act also formalizes the already evolving federal-state cooperative relationships in the civil rights field. It has long since been agreed that both federal and state authorities may legislate and enforce legislation in the field consistent with national constitutional standards. Under the new act, both governments are virtually required to work together in the enforcement stage. Federal authorities, in particular, are required to make every effort to cooperate with state and local authorities whenever they are forced to intervene at all.

Needless to say, conflict over this "treaty" and over the problems of enforcing antidiscrimination rulings generally is based primarily on a sectional division among the states with those of the old Confederacy aligned against the rest of their sisters, North and West. The one great interest alignment that cuts across state and sectional lines in this case is the obvious interest of most Negroes to achieve greater equality. There is also a cross-state alignment among those whites (almost invariably located outside the South) who actively support the Negro rights movement. Finally, there is a general predisposition on the part of those whites, North or South, who feel immediately threatened by government enforcement of Negro rights (for various reasons including those of constitutional construction) to oppose the thrust of any government action in this field.

There are some subconflicts generated within the states based on this one interest alignment. In the southern states, there are three subconflicts. The first and most important is between the Negroes and the authorities who resist Negro demands in the name of the white community. The second is among the whites between the moderates and the diehards. The moderates are basically urban cosmopolitans who, while generally opposed to integration (at least until recently), are more concerned with the continued development of their communities as parts of the national society than they are with the "threat" of Negro equality. In general, they are also less directly threatened by Negro gains. The diehards, both urban and rural, are usually locals, who place the race issue above all others in importance, primarily because they feel themselves to be directly threatened by any improvement in the Negroes' position.[17] The third conflict is within the

[17] The terms "cosmopolitans" and "locals" are used in their technical sense to denote particular frames of reference of different types of people represented in every community. For an elaboration of the concept embracing the two terms, see Robert K. Merton, "Patterns of Influence: Local and Cosmopolitan Influentials," in his *Social Theory and Social Structure*, 2d ed. (Glencoe, Ill.: The Free Press, 1957) and Daniel J. Elazar and Douglas St.

diehard ranks between those who advocate violent resistance—generally the lower-class "white trash" types—and those who advocate massive resistance that stops short of actual violence—generally the middle-class small town and small city "responsibles."

In the northern and western states, there are two subconflicts. Somewhat as in the South, the first and foremost is between the Negroes seeking to improve their lot plus a small sympathetic element in the white community and the bulk of the white community which is either apathetic or quietly hostile. Within the white community, the conflict is between those whose neighborhoods or patterns of business are likely to be broken by an influx of Negro residents and those who can afford to support the Negroes' demands without significant personal sacrifice. The former are generally the residents of older ethnic neighborhoods in large cities, while the latter are usually residents of suburbs, suburban-like neighborhoods within the cities, or areas with few or no Negroes.

Among the special considerations to be borne in mind in viewing the civil rights problem are (1) the changing interpretation of the intent of the Constitution in regard to the actual definition of what constitutes "equal rights" and the shifting locus of authority for enforcing the constitutional requirements; (2) the differences in state responses to the issue which make it a matter of federal-state conflict in a few states only; (3) the ability of the recalcitrant states as civil societies to resist and deflect actions taken against them or their citizens; (4) the self-imposed limitations which the federal government maintains because it has potentially overwhelming power and the reasons for such self-limitation; and (5) changes in public attitudes toward the problem or toward government action to deal with it which, in the long run, reduce its impact as a federal-state conflict.

Table 4 shows how the same framework can be used to analyze other kinds of issues. The *civil rights* issue may be described

Angelo, " 'Cosmopolitans' and 'Locals' in Contemporary Community Politics," *Proceedings of the Minnesota Academy of Science*, XXXI, 2 (1964), 171–178.

Table 4. Federalism and Nationwide Political Concerns: An Analytical Framework

Legislative Reapportionment

1. Essential Character

   Determines distribution of political power in state and national legislatures.

2. Authority and Power

   In flux.

   Originally legislative exclusively (state in state legislative apportionment, state and federal in congressional apportionment).

   Now apparently shifting from legislatures to sharing arrangement involving courts (state and federal) and legislatures.

   In matters of state legislative apportionment, originally a state concern; now apparently shifting to involve the judicial branch of the federal government.

3. Operational Relationships

   Conflict between legislatures (particularly state) and courts (particularly, but not exclusively, federal) for control.

4. Subconflicts

   Big city metropolitan interests vs. small metropolitan/small city /rural interests.

   Active-government advocates vs. restricted-government advocates.

5. State Alignments

   States generally opposed to U.S. Supreme Court assumption of authority.

   Change will be greatest in southern states.

   Scattering of states, particularly in the Northeast, in agreement with Court rulings.

6. Interest Alignments

   For court intervention:

   Liberal reformers.

   Big city leadership.

   Against court intervention:

   State legislative leadership.

   Political conservatives.

   System-oriented traditionalists (i.e., those who reject the right of the courts to intervene).

   Nonmetropolitan residents.

7. Special Considerations

   Common (and misleading) interpretation of the issue as primarily an urban-rural controversy.

Legislative Reapportionment (cont.)

The general problems of court intervention into legislative matters, constitutional interpretations, and judicial self-restraint.

The role of the U.S. Supreme Court as an umpire standing outside the system rather than as an agent of the national government interested in advancing federal control per se.

Rapid spread of an issue throughout the federal system because of action at the center.

Efforts to dilute court requirements politically in the U.S. Congress and in the state legislatures.

Federal Merit System Requirements and State Policy-making Officeholders

1. Essential Character

Conflict between federal program administrators and state executive officials over application of Hatch Act merit system requirements to appointed state policy-making offices.

2. Authority and Power: Concurrent

Federal:

Authority to set conditions for grants-in-aid.

Power to withdraw funds if conditions remain unmet.

State:

Authority to appoint officials and decide whether to accept federal aid.

Power to apply political pressure in Congress to prevent aid cutoff.

3. Operational Relationships

Generally cooperative between professionals engaged in routine administrative tasks.

4. Subconflicts

Program-oriented professionals at both levels vs. politicians.

5. State Alignments

States uniformly opposed to federal authority in this area.

6. Interest Alignments

None significant; internal government affair.

7. Special Considerations

Extent to which federal aid should bind gubernatorial appointments.

Use of federal "lever" by program-oriented professionals to take control of programs away from political generalists.

Virtually total absence of public interest in the issue.

Efforts of states to clarify situation through congressional action.

National Defense

1. Essential Character

   Maintenance of national security and, ultimately, national survival.

2. Authority and Power

   Authority constitutionally concurrent with final and preeminent authority lodged in federal government.

   Power predominantly federal; state power (through administration of National Guard and political influence in Congress) essentially secondary and interstitial.

3. Operational Relationships

   Predominantly federal, subject to state/local pressure through Congress.

   Exceptional programs—cooperative federal-state action.

4. Subconflicts (only those bearing in some measure on state-federal relationships)

   Location and maintenance of defense installations.

   Allocation of defense contracts.

   Federal "in lieu" tax payments for military lands.

   Defense-impact grants-in-aid.

   Local antagonisms toward service personnel or actions.

   National Guard vs. regular defense establishment.

   Interservice conflicts.

5. State Alignments

   Every state vitally interested in acquiring whatever it can for itself.

   Regional interstate cooperative arrangements to acquire greater share emerging in "have-not" sections.

   Some state support for alternate defense policies based on character of state's defense industry (e.g., California's support for manned bombers).

   Occasional state interest in immediate problem of its own military security (e.g., Florida vis-à-vis Cuba).

6. Interest Alignments (only those bearing in some measure on state-federal relationships)

   Competing civilian contractors and the programs they serve vs. alternate programs and the contractors they support.

   Interservice alignments.

   "Professional soldier" vs. state military establishments.

7. Special Considerations

   Obvious local impact of most defense expenditures and those defense activities conducted within the United States.

   The mobilization of the states' public and private resources and talents to maintain local interests in the defense program.

   The extent to which the perennial conflict between general

National Defense (cont.)
> policy and local interests is a real one and the extent to which general policies and local interests are compatible.
> Interstate competition for defense-related benefits.
> Private parties' use of local interest in economic development to promote their own advantage.

Public Assistance
1. Essential Character
> Broad-gauged complex of programs designed to maintain minimum level of economic security for American families.
2. Authority and Power: Shared
Federal:
> Authority to appropriate money for the general welfare and to set conditions for grants-in-aid.
> Power to raise and lower allocations, set formulas for distribution, and withdraw funds.

State:
> Authority to establish welfare programs, set conditions for recipients, supervise and control local authorities, accept or reject federal grants.
> Power to withdraw from federal programs, set internal welfare policies within broad limits, exceed federal standards.
3. Operational Relationships
> Cooperative operation of welfare programs by officials on all levels with minimum of conflict because of shared professional attitudes.
4. Subconflicts
> State legislatures vs. big cities over welfare needs and expenditures.
> Professional welfare workers vs. politicians over desirability and effects of welfare programs.
5. State Alignments
> Greater concern of highly urbanized states with public welfare programs.
> Special concern of "depressed area" states in federal aid.
> Tendency of less industrialized states to maintain minimum levels of assistance.
6. Interest Alignments
> Labor: prowelfare; business: neutral to skeptical.
> Symbolic prowelfare positions of liberals and antiwelfare positions of conservatives.

Public Assistance (cont.)
   "Senior citizens" as welfare lobby.
   Professional welfare workers as welfare lobby.
   Negroes prowelfare for civil rights reasons.
7. Special Considerations
   Achievement of widespread acceptance of welfare principle in
      last government.
   Practical devolution of policy-making as well as administration
      to the states.
   Role of professional welfare associations in setting nationwide
      policies and standards.
   Rise of new welfare problems (aging, rehabilitation, medicare)
      and their integration into the system.

---

as an essentially domestic concern that attracts a high level of
public attention because it reaches down to alter the very fabric
of the social order. *Legislative reapportionment* is a domestic concern that relates primarily to the distribution of political power
within the structure of government and attracts a very limited
amount of public attention. *The application of federal merit system regulations to appointed state officials at the policy-making
level* involved in programs partially supported by federal funds
is an issue of primary importance for the maintenance of the states'
internal autonomy which attracts virtually no public attention. The
concern with *national defense* has essentially an international
focus with domestic implications and, on its face, does not appear
to involve state-federal relations except marginally. It is considered
of crucial importance by political leaders and the public and attracts a high level of public attention in its major aspects. The
last, *public assistance* (welfare), is a domestic issue of specific
programmatic interest that relates primarily to the maintenance of
economic security for American families, nationwide, and which
attracts very little public attention except in crisis situations.

CHAPTER TWO

Politics and the Constitutional System

National Intervention and State Autonomy

Considering the continuous involvement of the states and the federal government in the same public concerns, we can ask three important questions: What are some of the ways in which the constitutional system and the politics it has developed operate to bring order out of the uncertainty that comes from dealing with nationwide concerns in an interlocking system of systems? How do those ways serve to strengthen the viability of the states as political systems by affecting the character of federal impacts upon them? How do they serve to weaken the states because they are parts of the national political system?

The answer to these questions lies in the very character of American federalism. In the American federal system, sharing of functions by all levels of government is and always has been the norm. As Morton Grodzins has said:

It is difficult to find any governmental activity which does not involve all three of the so-called "levels" of the federal system. In the most local of local functions—law enforcement or education, for example —the federal and state governments play important roles. In what, *a priori,* may be considered the purest central government activities— the conduct of foreign affairs, for example—the state and local governments have considerable responsibilities, directly and indirectly.[1]

Given the basic fact of sharing, it is impossible to talk about totally separate state and federal functions. At the same time, it is

[1] Morton Grodzins, "The Federal System," in *Goals for Americans* (Englewood Cliffs, N.J.: Prentice-Hall, 1960), p. 266.

clearly true that the ways in which functions are shared vary significantly from program to program. Moreover, as new issues are raised, debated, and then translated into concrete programs through the political process, sharing arrangements must be developed to work them into the overall fabric of the state-federal relationship.

One of the major political factors encouraging sharing is the ability of interests unable to gain satisfaction at one level of government to turn to another in an effort to better their fortunes. We have noted how states, when their citizens stand together, can function as civil societies even in opposition to national demands. We have also noted that few issues confronting the American people have so great an impact on the states as to unite their people in a common front. This means that, in most cases, issues will lead to conflicts dividing the states as well as the nation. In terms of federalism, this often means that people unable to gain satisfaction from their state governments directly will turn to seek outside assistance from whatever source available. Sometimes such appeals are made to local government, but more frequently the interested parties turn to Washington. If the issue and the hour are right, then their appeal will be answered, often redounding upon the states with great force to alter the internal balance of political forces within them. In a real sense, this has been the history of reform in the United States, and since reform is one of the nation's fundamental recurring phenomena, the very character of the federal system has depended upon the way in which its components have been able to respond to such pressures and maneuvers.

Federal assumption of new formal responsibilities is most likely to occur when substantial majorities within a majority of the states have come to advocate or accept the necessity for a particular program or course of action which their state governments will not adopt or, as is most frequently the case, cannot adopt alone. Where there are popular majorities in a majority of the states and the state governments do not act, it usually means they cannot, willing as they might be to support the programs in question.

Given the existence of a national economy in which people and goods flow across boundaries with ease on the basis of essentially private decisions, the state governments, no matter how willing, are simply unable to cope with certain problems without federal assistance. Unemployment insurance, workmen's compensation, water pollution control, major highway construction, and a whole host of programs cannot be undertaken alone, even by those states that can afford to support them. The nation's great industrial corporations have facilities in too many different states, sell their goods in all the rest, and can locate (or relocate) their operations as they see fit. The nation's great waterways—and, by connection, most of its smaller ones—flow across state lines, carrying with them whatever is deposited upstream. The nation's highways can only service the nationwide market if they provide for easy transitions from jurisdiction to jurisdiction. In all these cases, state action to exercise legitimate controls, to set appropriate standards, or to implement public programs must, at the very least, be supported by federal actions or policies that will give the states room in which to maneuver. In such cases, federal assistance almost invariably acts to reenforce the administrative or policy-making powers of the state governments vis-à-vis the interests that lobby before them, supporting rather than interfering with them as civil societies.

The history of federal involvement in the regulation of interstate commerce is a case in point. With the consolidation of smaller railroad and manufacturing companies into larger interstate systems after the Civil War, the state governments found that they could not unilaterally mobilize sufficient power to regulate wealthy railroads that could cut them off from the rest of the country in retaliation, or deal with great industrial combines that could pull up stakes and go elsewhere, particularly in face of hostile rulings by the United States Supreme Court. Congress alone had the power to deflect the Court's intentions and master the great corporations in the name of the public interest. Federal intervention, when it finally came, actually strengthened the ability of the states to deal with the problems generated by these enterprises within their boundaries.

On a different level, most states have never been able to finance the great water resource projects undertaken within their limits, even if they are the principal beneficiaries of erstwhile federal "intervention" to construct them. In case after case, they have mobilized as civil societies to seek federal assistance without regarding such aid as destructive of their integrity as states. Or, in yet another kind of problem, until the federal government made it advantageous for all states to adopt unemployment compensation programs, those that wished to do so were handicapped by threats of major employers to move elsewhere.[2]

There are times, however, when minorities within the states turn to the federal government for assistance. The minority appeal "outward" is a phenomenon found most frequently in states divided between dominant and minority political subcultures (see Chapter Four), but also in any state divided into two or more camps on matters of policy. The possibility for this kind of appeal is one of the things that makes it difficult for the states to maintain an autonomous *politics* unaffected by national currents in their "domestic" decisions even though they can maintain reasonably autonomous *political systems*. The autonomy of their political systems may allow the states to bend in the face of blows from the outside and to recover more or less intact after their initial impact (a phenomenon not to be minimized), but it does not necessarily enable them to prevent outside blows in the first place.

The example of the public welfare reformers is perhaps classic in this respect. During the first decades of the twentieth century, reform groups working within the states sought to drastically enlarge state and local public welfare programs to cope

[2] William Anderson discusses this point at length in *The Nation and the States, Rivals or Partners?* (Minneapolis: University of Minnesota Press, 1955).

with the dislocations incident to an industrial society. After some initial successes in the regulatory field, the reformers were generally rebuffed in their efforts to secure positive welfare measures partly because their proposed programs were expensive and state legislatures did not wish to raise taxes, partly because the interests generally dominant in the states (and in the nation as a whole) opposed such programs, and partly because interstate economic competition made it difficult for most states to enact such measures unilaterally. After repeated failures, the reformers began to intensify their efforts to gain federal assistance for their programs without abandoning their efforts at the state level. The change in economic conditions brought by the Great Depression made possible the enactment of the programs they advocated. A system of federal grants was introduced to stimulate the creation of basic welfare programs in every state under minimal national standards and to share in supporting those programs. Given this federal assistance, the welfare reformers were able to gain control over the new programs in virtually all the states except those in which unsympathetic political organizations were too strong and there were no significant indigenous groups of welfare reformers ready to take over. Federal grants replaced "bread and coal basket politics" as a major instrument of party organization and at least temporarily weakened traditional political machines, opening the way for reform groups to act on a number of fronts. Federal merit system requirements administered by the reformers in many states broke the back of state patronage systems in most welfare departments, opening the door for professional welfare workers to assume basic responsibility for the operation of even general relief programs. The increased funds available to each state encouraged the development of more sophisticated administrative organizations in political systems long noted for resistance to bureaucratization.

These and other changes meant that state politics had to be readjusted so that the state political systems could assimilate the new demands placed upon them. In fact, the states made that adjustment rapidly, influencing the shaping of the new programs every step of the way. None remained outside the programs or unaffected by them.[3]

Today urban reformers interested in reconstructing America's cities are following much the same course of action. They have turned to Washington for aid unobtainable from most of the states in the hope, among others, that through Washington they will become powerful in their respective state capitols as well. There is every indication they will succeed in their efforts, at least to the extent the welfare reformers did a generation ago.

This ability of unsatisfied and even disaffected interests to turn elsewhere adds a certain element of uncertainty to the internal politics of every state, an uncertainty that frequently has considerable value in enabling the American political system to adjust to changing circumstances and new public needs. Yet left unchecked, this very uncertainty could reduce the federal system to meaninglessness and the states to little more than ciphers. Ultimately, what prevents it from doing so is public support for the system as it stands. More tangibly, it is the system's constitutional base which keeps it a system of systems. Central to this constitutional base is the Constitution itself, which acts upon the ordinary whirl of politics as a conservative brake to restrain its centripetal effects.

Thus, while many of the urban reformers may not care whether the federal government seeks to involve the states and federal aid programs or not, the existence of the Constitution demands state participation. At the very least, the states must pass

[3] For a good history of the reformers' activities at the state and national level in this period, see Arthur Schlesinger, Jr.'s trilogy, "The Age of Roosevelt," particularly volumes one and two, *The Crisis of the Old Order* (Boston: Houghton Mifflin, 1957) and *The Coming of the New Deal* (Boston: Houghton Mifflin, 1959). The reformers were by no means immediately successful, even in states highly sympathetic to their long-range goals. Paul Ylvisaker's case study of the effort to professionalize the local welfare directorship in Blue Earth County, Minnesota, in the late 1930's is a good example of the struggle that was needed to change established political patterns even in a state favorably disposed to public welfare programs and the merit system. It is also an excellent study of local influence in the federal system. See *The Battle of Blue Earth County*, Committee on Public Administration Cases, 1950.

enabling legislation before any of their cities can participate in federal aid programs or take federal funds. In most cases, the federal legislation is drawn—by men who respect the Constitution—to either require state participation or at least give the states the choice as to whether they participate actively. Thus the impetus for political change, which is no respecter of institutions, is brought to heel by the constitutional base, to the great benefit of the states as political systems.[4]

When we speak of "the constitutional base," we speak of more than the formal document itself. Included within the meaning of that term is the bundle of basic texts and statutes, court decisions, accepted constitutional interpretations, maintained customs and institutional traditions that have been combined with the written document to become "the Constitution" supported by the American public consensus. When we speak of the role of the Constitution in bringing a certain degree of order out of the chaos generated by nationwide involvement in universal concerns, we refer not only to the immediate role of the constitutional base, but to the larger impact of the constitutional structure on electoral behavior, the party system, the role of interest groups—in short, its impact on the other major elements of the American political system.

The Constitutional Place of the States

The constitutional place of the states in the federal system is determined by four kinds of material: the provisions in the federal and state constitutions that either limit or guarantee the powers of the states vis-à-vis the federal government; the provisions in those constitutions which give the states a role in the composition of the national government; the subsequent interpretations of both sets of provisions by the courts (particularly the United States Supreme Court); and the unwritten constitutional traditions which have evolved informally and have only later

[4] Morton Grodzins describes this procedure in "American Political Parties and the American System," *Western Political Quarterly*, XIII (December 1960), 974–998.

been formally recognized through the first three, directly or indirectly.

The precise federal constitutional provisions outlining the general position of the states must always be taken into consideration even if some of them can be transcended through politics in specific situations. Table 5 deals with specific limitations and guarantees of state powers. These limitations and guarantees fall into four basic categories: general concern with the integrity of the states as well as their subordination to the Union; some brief provisions insuring the states a role in the common defense; a delineation of the role of the states in the two central areas of positive governmental activity at home, management of commerce and raising of revenues; and a description of state responsibilities in the administration of justice. Table 6 outlines the role that must be played by the states if the federal government is to function and clarifies the constitutional limits of that role.

The state constitutions are generally silent regarding state-federal relationships. When they speak at all, it is essentially to ratify the requirements of the federal constitution by making them applicable to specific local situations. Most state constitutions formally delineate their inviolable borders. In the constitu-

Table 5. Federal Constitutional Provisions Specifically Guaranteeing or Limiting State Powers

GUARANTEES	LIMITS
A. STATE INTEGRITY AND SOVEREIGNTY	
No division or consolidation of states without state legislative consent (IV-2) ᵃ	States cannot enter into treaties, alliances, or confederations (I-10)
Republican form of government (IV-2)	No separate coinage (I-10)
Protection against invasion (IV-2)	No grants of titles of nobility (I-10)
Protection against domestic violence on application of proper state authorities (IV-2)	No interstate or foreign compacts without congressional consent (I-10)
Powers not delegated to the U.S.	Constitution, all laws and treaties made under it to be supreme law

GUARANTEES	LIMITS

GUARANTEES	LIMITS
by Constitution, nor prohibited by it to the states, are reserved to the states (Amend. X)	of the land, binding on every state (VI)
	Slavery forbidden (Amend. XIII)
States cannot be sued by citizens of another state or a foreign nation (Amend. XI)	All state legislative, executive, and judicial officers and state representatives in Congress to be bound by Constitution (VI)
	No abridgment of privileges and immunities of U.S. citizens (Amend. XIV)
	Reduction of representation in House of Representatives for denial of franchise to citizens (Amend. XIV)
	No payment of debts incurred in aid of insurrection or rebellion against U.S. or for emancipation of slaves (Amend. XIV)
	No abridgment of right to vote on account of race, color, or previous condition of servitude (Amend. XV)
	Popular election of senators (Amend. XVII)
	No abridgment of right to vote on account of sex (Amend. XIX)
	No poll taxes in federal elections (Amend. XXIV)

B. MILITARY AFFAIRS AND DEFENSE

GUARANTEES	LIMITS
Power to maintain militia and appoint militia officers (I-8, Amend. II)	No letters of marque and reprisal (I-10)
	No maintenance of standing military forces in peacetime without congressional consent (I-10)
	No engagement in war without congressional consent, except to repel invasion (I-10)

[41]

GUARANTEES	LIMITS

C. COMMERCE AND TAXATION

Equal apportionment of direct federal taxes (I-2, 9)

No federal export duties (I-9)

No preferential treatment for ports of one state (I-9)

Reciprocal full faith and credit among states for public acts, records, and judicial proceedings (IV-1)

Reciprocal privileges and immunities for citizens of the several states (IV-2)

Intoxicating liquor may not be imported into states where its sale or use is prohibited (Amend. XXI-2)

No levying of duties on vessels of sister states (I-9)

No legal tender other than gold or silver (I-10)

No impairment of obligations of contracts (I-10)

No levying of import or export duties without consent of Congress except reasonable inspection fees (I-10)

No tonnage duties without congressional consent (I-10)

D. ADMINISTRATION OF JUSTICE

Federal criminal trials to be held in state where crime was committed (III-2) [b]

Extradition for crimes (IV-2)

Federal criminal juries to be chosen from state and district in which crime was committed (Amend. VI) [b]

Federal judicial power to extend to controversies between two or more states; between a state and citizens of another state when state is plaintiff, and between foreign nation or its citizens, with original jurisdiction vested in the Supreme Court (III-2)

No bills of attainder (I-10)

No ex post facto laws (I-10)

Supreme Court has original jurisdiction over all cases in which a state shall be a party (III-2)

Judges in every state bound by Constitution and all laws and treaties made under it, notwithstanding the constitutions or laws of any state (VI)

No denial of life, liberty, or property without due process of law (Amend. XIV)

No denial of equal protection of state laws to persons within its limits (Amend. XIV)

---

[a] Numbers in parentheses refer to the article and section of the Constitution containing the provision.

[b] This provision insures the integrity of the state's common law in federal cases.

Table 6. Federal Constitutional Provisions Specifically Giving the States a Role in the Composition of the National Government

GUARANTEES	LIMITS
A. NATIONAL LEGISLATURE	
Members of House of Representatives chosen by voters, those qualified to vote for most numerous house of state legislature in the several states (I-2) [a]	Representatives must be 25 years old and citizens of the U.S. for 7 years (I-2)
At time of election, representatives must be inhabitants of states from which they are elected (1-2)	Senators must be 30 years old and citizens of the U.S. for 9 years (I-3)
Representatives to be apportioned among the states according to population every 10 years (I-2)	Congress may make or alter regulations as to the times, places, and manner of holding elections for senators and representatives (I-4)
State executive has authority to fill vacancies (I-2)	Each house shall be the judge of the elections, returns, and qualifications of its own members, shall punish its members for disorderly behavior, and shall expel a member by two-thirds vote (I-5)
Each state shall have at least one representative (I-2)	
Senate shall be composed of two senators from each state (I-3) chosen by the people qualified to vote for the most numerous house of the state legislature (Amend. XVII), with vacancies to be filled as prescribed by state legislation (Amend. XVII)	Basis for apportionment of representation in House of Representatives may be reduced proportionate to state deprivation of the right to vote of otherwise qualified citizens (Amend. XIV-2)
At time of election, senators must be inhabitants of the states from which they are chosen (I-3)	Without express consent of two-thirds of Congress, states cannot be represented by persons who have taken an oath to support the Constitution and have since engaged in insurrection (Amend. XIV-3)
Times, places, and manner of holding elections for senators and representatives shall be prescribed for each state by its legislature (I-4)	
No state to be deprived of equal representation in the Senate without its consent (V)	

B. NATIONAL EXECUTIVE

To be selected by the electors of the several states with each state allotted a number of electors equal to the total number of its senators and representatives (II-1)

Each state to have one vote if presidential election is decided in House of Representatives (II-1)

Approval of presidential appointees by the Senate as Congress shall prescribe (II-2)

Congress may determine the time of choosing electors and a uniform day on which they shall cast their votes (II-1)

C. AMENDMENT OF CONSTITUTION

Amendments must be ratified by three-fourths of the states (V)

Amendments must be proposed by two-thirds of the states (V)

D. VOTING RIGHTS

Cannot be denied or abridged on grounds of race, color, or previous condition of servitude (Amend. XV-1)

Cannot be denied or abridged on account of sex (Amend. XIX-1)

No poll tax may be levied as requirement to vote in federal elections (Amend. XXIV)

E. FOREIGN AFFAIRS

Treaties must be ratified by two-thirds of Senate (II-2)

Appointment of foreign service officers subject to Senate confirmation (II-2)

Treaties binding on states as supreme law of the land (VI)

F. MILITARY AFFAIRS AND DEFENSE

Power to appoint the officers of and train the militia when not in

Congress may provide for organizing, arming, and disciplining

F. MILITARY AFFAIRS AND DEFENSE (*cont.*)

federal service reserved to the states (I-8)	the militia when it is not in federal service and for governing it when it is (I-8)

ᵃ Numbers in parentheses refer to the article and section of the Constitution containing the provision.

tions of the public-land states (created under the tutelage of the federal government after the adoption of the United States Constitution), provisions governing the commitment of federal land grants for specific public purposes serve as a formal acknowledgment of the federal-state partnership that had become important as early as 1802 when Ohio, the first state of this group, adopted its first constitution.[5] The provisions of the Minnesota constitution are typical. The 1857 federal enabling act authorizing Minnesota's admission to statehood sets forth the prospective state's boundaries; the extent of its jurisdiction over the rivers setting its boundaries; federal land grants for common schools, a university, public buildings, salt springs, and internal improvements; and the conditions governing the use of these land grants and their proceeds. The state constitution adopted in 1858 includes provisions setting forth the state's boundaries (Article II, Sec. 1) and jurisdiction (Article II, Sec. 2) in the terms of the enabling act, and a general provision (Article II, Sec. 3) incorporating all the rest of the enabling act's conditions.

The constitutions of the reconstructed southern states were redrawn to include specific acknowledgments of federal supremacy and abjurations of the "right" of succession as a requirement for their restoration, as in the North Carolina constitution:

Art. I, Sec. 4. *That there is no right to secede.* That this State shall ever remain a member of the American Union; that the people thereof are a part of the American Nation; that there is no right on the part of the State to secede, and that all attempts, from whatever source or

[5] See Daniel J. Elazar, *The American Partnership* (Chicago: University of Chicago Press, 1962), Part Two.

upon whatever pretext, to dissolve said Union or to sever said Nation, ought to be resisted with the whole power of the State.

Art. I, Sec. 5. *Of allegiance to the United States Government.* That every citizen of this State owes paramount allegiance to the Constitution and Government of the United States, and that no law or ordinance of the State in contravention or subversion thereof can have any binding force.

Art. I, Sec. 6. . . . The State shall never assume or pay, or authorize the collection of any debt or obligation, express or implied, incurred in aid of insurrection or rebellion against the United States, or any claim for the loss or emancipation of any slave . . .

While these constitutions offer the most clear-cut statement of the place of the states in the Union to be found in any state constitutional documents, they merely spell out similar provisions found in several of the state constitutions of the Revolutionary era.

The Constitution and the New Politics

Whatever the American constitutional base may mean in legal terms, in behavioral terms it can be understood as the mediating force between the pressures of politics found universally in all political systems and the particular federal structure of politics peculiar to the United States. In fact, the character of the American federal system is maintained and made functional only partly by immediate constitutional requirements. While the role of such requirements should not be minimized, most important is the way in which the institutions and purposes of federalism are made through the political process. At the same time, it was the special nature of the American constitutional system, so unique when it emerged in the late eighteenth century, that gave rise to the "new politics" which we now take for granted as the politics of democratic government.

Federalism as we know it was the invention of the founders of the United States, a product of their immediate experiences in the British Empire and the work of Revolutionary assemblies. The originators of American federalism drew upon several fundamental ideas which had been developed by the seventeenth- and eighteenth-century formulators of the new political science, particularly Hobbes, Locke, James Harrington, and Montesquieu. Among these ideas were such modern theoretical prerequisites of Federalism as the idea of the constitution as a humanly willed compact which could be humanly altered; the notion of popular sovereignty (as distinct from sovereignty vested in a single superior person), which makes it possible for two or more governments to share the attributes of sovereignty without altering the indivisibility of sovereignty; and the idea of fragmented-yet-coordinated government, which permits the distribution of power among different governmental institutions to prevent its abuse without creating a concomitant loss of the ability to concentrate certain kinds of power for purposes of governing.

By accepting the notion of a noncentralized government based on a system of systems and writing that notion into the fundamental structure of American government, the founders of the United States created the need for the development of a new politics to make their new constitution operational. The tasks of this new politics were twofold: to maintain the division of powers among governments in the face of national pressures toward centralization or local pressures toward fragmentation, and to provide a means for mobilizing power within the noncentralized system to make effective government of the nation and the states possible. Both these tasks have remained vital and necessary in the context of American politics. Taken together they well express the central role of federalism in solving a major problem of popular government, namely, how to maintain the liberties of the people from vitiation through the consolidation of power into hands far removed from popular control or domination of minorities by an unrestrained majority, while at the same time providing a government with sufficient energy to meet the demands placed upon it.[6]

[6] As the founders of the American Republic well knew, the ultimate justification of federalism lies in its ability to combine these elements to actively protect liberty and diversity within democratic government operating to establish justice under law. This point cannot be amplified here, but the interested reader is urged to explore it further in *The Federalist*, which remains the best discussion of the problem and its federal solution. Martin

The Political Process and
Intergovernmental Collaboration

The political process generated by the "new politics" affects the state-federal relationship most directly as it is funneled through three basic political channels: territorial democracy, a dual legal system, and the political parties.

Partly because of the traditions of federalism and partly because of the heritage of an agrarian society, the basic pattern of political organization in the United States is territorial. That is to say, American politics is formally organized around units of territory rather than economic or ethnic groups, social classes, or the like. The nation is divided into states, the states are divided into counties, the counties include townships, cities, and special districts, and the whole country is divided into election districts of varying sizes ranging from congressional districts to precincts. This means that people and their interests gain formal representation in the councils of government through the location of various interests in particular places and their ability to capture political control of territorial political units. In many ways this is the most neutral kind of representation. As soon as one interest declines in importance and a new one rises, it can gain some voice in the system because the people who reflect that interest are located in some particular political subdivision and can vote there. This neutrality of territory has reenforced the notion of territorial democracy so that it remains the fundamental basis for political representation even in the highly urbanized American society of today.[7]

A second basic channel is the multiple system of laws and

Diamond provides an excellent analysis of the immediate intentions of the framers of the Constitution in *"The Federalist's* View of Federalism," in *Essays in Federalism* (Claremont, Calif.: Institute for Studies in Federalism, 1961), pp. 21–64.

[7] Little has been written about the concept of territorial democracy in recent years. Russell Kirk presents one view of this aspect of federalism in Robert Goldwin, ed., *A Nation of States* (Chicago: Rand McNally, 1962).

courts tied to the federal division of powers. In the nation as a whole, state law is the basic law. There is no federal common law. Rather, federal law is limited in scope, and the common law is interpreted on a state by state basis. This means that both state and federal courts are bound by state-made law unless it is superseded by the Constitution or federal statutory law. Federal statutory law is essentially designed to fill in the gaps left by the existence of fifty different legal systems. Two noted authorities have described the situation concisely:

Federal law is generally interstitial in its nature. It rarely occupies a legal field completely . . . despite the volumes of Congressional enactments, and even within areas where Congress has been very active. Federal legislation, on the whole, has been conceived and drafted on an *ad hoc* basis to accomplish limited objectives. It builds upon legal relationships established by the states, altering or supplanting them only so far as necessary for the special purpose. Congress acts, in short, against the background of the total *corpus juris* of the states in much the same way that a state legislature acts against the background of the common law, assumed to govern unless changed by legislation.[8]

The complexity of this system of systems is compounded by the nature of the dual court structure, with each state and the federal government having its own complete court system. The federal courts stand in a somewhat superior relationship to the state courts in a widening variety of ways. Led by the United States Supreme Court, which is constitutionally placed at the apex of both court systems, the federal courts interpret federal law, review the work of the state courts, and enforce the laws of the states in which they are located in cases that come under federal jurisdiction.

The third basic political channel is the party system. The Democratic and Republican parties represent two broad confederations of otherwise largely independent state party organizations which unite on the national level, primarily to gain public office. Despite the greater public attention given the national

[8] Henry M. Hart, Jr., and Herbert Wechsler, *The Federal Courts and the Federal System* (Brooklyn, N.Y.: Foundation Press, 1953), p. 435.

parties, the real centers of party organization, finance, and power are at the state and local levels. This noncentralization of the parties contributes to the maintenance of generally noncentralized government in the United States and to the perpetuation of a high degree of local control even in the face of "big government." Thus the party system is of great importance in maintaining the basic structure of American politics and basic American political values, including those of federalism.

The parties are important in recruiting, nominating, and electing candidates to all national and most state offices. They are somewhat less important in electing officials at the local level, where nonpartisan elections are popular. But even where party support is important for election, public officials are not responsible to their parties but to their constituencies (territorial democracy). Consequently party discipline is minimal and most elected officials are free to respond to the pressures of their constituents, or to the pressures of the interests that are strong in their constituencies, before having to respond to the demands of party. This situation is so well entrenched that the parties have made a virtue out of necessity and have structured their operations with it in mind.

The party system has become the organizing principle around which national and state politics (and federalism itself) have been able to develop, even to the point of interposing itself between the Constitution and the courts in determining the respective roles of the federal government and the states. The American political parties rarely centralize power at all. Characteristically they do the reverse, serving as a canopy under which special and local interests are represented with little regard for anything that can be called a party program. Moreover, party operations play a major role in producing, through Congress, the basic division of functions between the federal government and state and local governments at any given moment in history, transforming the Supreme Court's well-known permissiveness with respect to the expansion of national powers into legislation that characteristically provides important roles for state and local governments.[9]

The party system, like federalism itself, stands in the anomalous position of being fundamental to the functioning of Amercan government, yet rarely visible as a direct means of achieving political goals. Without party discipline to make party voting important in legislative matters, without clear-cut ideological differences between the two parties to make party lines important, it often seems as if the party system were a mere appendage in American politics. Yet the parties represent organizing institutions that bring unity across potentially troublesome cleavages, just as the existence of the states provides a means to handle diversity with the neutrality that comes of territorial representation.[10]

The major effect of the expansion of the role of politics as a means of modifying the Constitution has been to increase the level of intergovernmental collaboration. It has provided means for interests to successfully make demands on the federal government while at the same time insuring that the federal response is guided by a solicitude for the position of the states. This solicitude has meant that federal action usually reenforces the actions of the states and, at the very least, provides for their participation in some way.

[9] Grodzins, "American Political Parties and the American System."

[10] This aspect of the role of political parties is described in Austin Ranney and Willmore Kendall, *Democracy and the American Party System* (New York: Harcourt, Brace & World, 1956).

CHAPTER THREE

The Partnership in Action

The Scope of Sharing

In the years since the establishment of the Republic, intergovernmental collaboration has been progressively expanded to include virtually every governmental function. From public welfare to public recreation, from national defense to local police protection, the system of sharing has become so pervasive that it is often difficult for the uninitiated bystander to tell just who is doing what under which hat.[1] The highly institutionalized system of federal-state cooperation which has developed has become part of the nation's constitutional tradition. Under this cooperative system, the federal government, the states, and the localities share the burden for the great domestic programs by making the larger governments primarily responsible for raising revenues and setting standards, and the smaller ones primarily responsible for administering the programs. For each program, all governments involved contribute toward making policy in ways which often depend upon the forms of sharing involved.

The state-federal mixture of responsibility and activity in serving the nation's "great constituencies"—Agriculture, Business, and Labor—clearly illustrates the extent to which sharing has become routine and institutionalized. Table 7 shows how this is so in the major areas of concern for each.

[1] For a complete and analytical description of the involved nature of intergovernmental collaboration, see Morton Grodzins, *The American System: A New View of Government in the United States,* ed. Daniel J. Elazar (Chicago: Rand McNally, 1966).

The Constitution itself requires state-federal cooperation in some fields (administration of elections, for example) and makes cooperation in others possible by giving both governments broad concurrent powers. Since 1790, the courts, Congress, and custom have virtually eliminated all possible restrictions on joint federal-state action, even while generally reaffirming the necessity for separate sets of political institutions for each. Where concurrent jurisdiction was clearly constitutional, it has been sustained, and where the issue was in doubt, concurrent powers have been extended.[2]

This trend has often been viewed as a simple expansion of federal power at the expense of the states. In reality, it has meant an expansion of the realm of activities of both federal and state governments to generate an increase in the velocity of government (that is, the amount of governmental activity in relation to the total activity of society) in the nation as a whole. Thus the acts of Congress have tended to give the states a firm share in virtually all federal domestic programs, including several in which the federal government is apparently given the right to claim exclusive jurisdiction in the words of the Constitution itself. For example, the improvement of navigable waters was to be a federal responsibility under the Constitution. In practice, it has become a joint responsibility involving the federal government,

Table 7. The Mixture of Federal-State Activity in Serving the Great Constituencies

---

I. BUSINESS

A. Establishing Favorable Conditions

1. Protection of private property rights	States have primary responsibility; federal govt. has limited role
2. Establishment of organizational forms for business enterprise	
3. Establishing rules of bankruptcy and business reorganization	Shared responsibility

[2] Carl B. Swisher, *The Growth of Constitutional Power in the United States,* rev. ed. (Chicago: University of Chicago Press, 1963) presents a brief, analytical history of the trend.

4. Granting patent rights	Federal responsibility
5. Maintaining a monetary system	

B. Direct Aids
1. Tariffs — Federal aid
2. Price supports

3. Industrial subsidies — Shared aid: federal share generally larger
4. Data-gathering and economic studies
5. Money- or credit-lending

C. Regulation
1. Maintenance of competition — Shared: federal role larger
2. Transportation regulation
3. Atomic energy regulation
4. Regulating banking, bank credit, bank deposits
5. Protecting investors

6. Licensing ordinary business — State responsibility

7. Utility regulation — Shared

8. Regulation of communications — Federal responsibility; states have minor role

II. LABOR

A. Protection against Exploitation
1. Limiting child labor — Shared responsibility with federal share larger
2. Protecting women workers
3. Limiting hours of work
4. Establishing minimum wages

5. Preventing racial and religious discrimination — Primarily state responsibility with federal share growing
6. Protecting migratory labor

7. Compensation for injuries on the job — State responsibility supported by federal action

B. Protection of Right to Organize and Bargain Collectively
    1. Protecting right to organize   Shared responsibil-
    2. Protecting right to strike   ity; federal share
    3. Providing mechanisms for settling la-   larger
       bor-management disputes

C. Assistance in Finding and Keeping Jobs
    1. Providing employment offices   Shared responsibil-
    2. Stimulating employment opportunities   ity: states have pri-
    3. Assisting in manpower retraining   mary role; federal
    4. Providing unemployment compensa-   government in sup-
       tion   porting role

III. AGRICULTURE

A. Increasing Productivity
    1. Managing research   Shared: states have
    2. Diffusing knowledge   primary role with
    3. Providing technical assistance   federal support

    4. Developing field projects   Shared equally

B. Maintaining Commodity Prices
    1. Insuring parity and supporting prices   Largely federal with
    2. Regulating production   state support
    3. Acquiring and storing surpluses

C. Regulating Quality of Produce
    1. Sanitary inspection   Shared
    2. Health inspection
    3. Grading and quality inspection

D. Developing Agricultural Markets
    1. Securing tariff concessions   Federal responsibil-
       ity

    2. Disposing of the stored agricultural   Primarily federal
       surplus

    3. Promoting product use   Primarily state

    4. Opening new markets   Shared

the states, and their local subdivisions in cooperative projects. By the same token, policing the waters, originally a state and local responsibility, has come to involve the United States Coast Guard as well.

In some cases, Congress has even "overruled" the Supreme Court and turned functions given it by judicial interpretation over to the states. Ownership of the submerged oil lands, regulation of the insurance business, and preemptive powers in the field of labor legislation are cases in point. In all three instances, the Supreme Court ruled that federal authority was preeminent and in all three Congress ceded all or part of that authority back to the states.[3]

If the federal system were predicated on a clean separation of functions as well as structure (i.e., dual federalism), then centralization would probably have been inevitable when it became necessary for the federal government to intervene in problems that by their very nature transcended state lines. In fact, federal intervention could be supplementary and stimulatory rather than preemptive because of the possibilities for intergovernmental collaboration.

Since federal involvement in any given program has often come before substantial state involvement, there are few cases of federal expansion at the expense of ongoing state operations. In most cases, while the states may have had the authority to act from the first, historically only a few have taken the initiative in exercising that authority. Thus, in reality, federal involvement has usually served to stimulate the states' exercise of their own powers, encouraging a great expansion of state activity in the same fields and an overall enlargement of the scope of state governmental operations. Such expansion has not only meant greater state expenditure of funds but also an increase in the number and quality of the

---

[3] The tidelands oil case is particularly interesting as it generated a tremendous amount of controversy, with the states lining up on both sides. For a history of the case, see Ernest R. Bartley, *The Tidelands Oil Controversy: A Legal and Historical Analysis* (Austin: University of Texas Press, 1953) and *Congress and the Nation, 1945–1964* (Washington: Congressional Quarterly Service, 1965), pp. 1401–1404.

personnel involved in carrying out the states' operations. The de-velopment of cadres of professionals at the state level has led, in turn, to an increase in the states' ability to make policy for the internal operation of cooperative programs and often to make their policy decisions stick even in the face of occasional federal opposition.

Take today's state-federal welfare programs, which were considered such radical attempts at centralization in the 1930's. We commonly think of these great grant programs as Federal (meaning national, coming-out-of-Washington) programs. Yet in reality they are federal (meaning shared-by-Washington-and-the-states) programs with the emphasis for shaping them increasingly placed on the states. While Washington sets certain basic standards for each welfare program, it is actually the province of the states not only to administer those programs which their legislatures have authorized within their boundaries, but to determine a major share of the welfare policy they will follow. Within certain limits, the states determine the size of welfare payments and the eligibility for different forms of assistance, while Congress, according to a preset formula (approximately but not exactly fifty-fifty, depending on the program), guarantees to match the state expenditures, no matter how large they may be. Indeed, if Congress has not appropriated enough money to cover the federal share, it must, by law, make the necessary deficiency appropriations. The federal administrators oversee the transfer of funds and audit their use but do little to interfere with the operations of state welfare programs.[4]

The extent of state control over these programs was nowhere better illustrated than in a recent welfare crisis in Illinois. Faced with mounting welfare costs, the governor and general assembly tried to cut down the number of cases on the welfare rolls, particularly in the Chicago area, and to put ceilings on individual welfare payments. Their efforts led, on a least two occasions, to the

---

[4] A description of this relationship is available in the report on *Twenty-five Grant-in-Aid Programs,* submitted to the Commission on Intergovernmental Relations (Washington: Government Printing Office, 1955).

temporary suspension of all welfare payments in Cook County (Chicago). In both cases, federal welfare officials, though active behind the scenes in efforts to restore payments, were basically powerless to intervene (other than to provide some surplus commodities for city officials to distribute), even though federal funds covered half the cost of the programs involved. The most extreme punishment provided by federal law is the withdrawal of federal funds from state programs that do not meet federal standards, but Congress has never looked with kindness upon the use of this punishment. Besides, its use in this case would hardly have helped achieve the primary aim—resumption of payments—and even if the federal officials had cared to use it, they would have risked incurring the wrath of the political forces that made it possible for them to stay in business in the first place. They undoubtedly knew that past attempts to revoke federal aid funds in any program had virtually all failed. So the problem in each case was ultimately resolved within the state's political system through the efforts of Illinois citizens, the great majority of whom were no more desirous of stopping the welfare programs than were the federal welfare officials.[5]

In the cooperative highway programs, in most public health programs, in the cooperative agricultural programs, indeed, in the entire body of the great grant programs presently in operation, situations similar to that in Illinois have occurred with a similar reliance upon state and local interests to resolve them. It would be misleading, however, to think of the shared aspects of these programs as producing a residue of state-local obstructionism politically powerful enough to defeat enlightened federal administrators. As in the Illinois welfare case, there is no significant inter-level disagreement as to the virtue of the programs in question, only differences of opinion as to specific policies or methods of administration.

[5] The writer observed this case personally. What impressed him most about the manner of its resolution was the way in which the problem was treated by the politicians and the public as a purely internal affair, a matter to be decided by citizens of Illinois without serious reference to the federal government as a participant in any way.

Unfortunately, the more spectacular examples of the power of the states within the cooperative framework tend to reflect obstructionism (or something akin to it). The Negro rights problem is clearly a case in point. In the less publicized problems of highway construction, public health, conservation, and the like, and in the routines of day-to-day collaboration common to every program, there is generally little conflict between levels of government. When such conflict does erupt, as frequently as not the power of the states is used to advance projects commonly considered in the public interest against what might be called federal shortsightedness. Governor Nelson Rockefeller has related a good example of this. New York State wished to acquire certain surplus military lands within its boundaries for park purposes. The federal General Services Administration put a high price tag on the land, primarily to gain greater return for the federal treasury, a mission pursued singlemindedly by the GSA. Certain private developers were interested in acquiring the lands for subdivision and were willing to meet the price. The state officials, who felt that the lands should be made available to New York at reduced cost since they were to be used for public purposes, arranged to have the lands zoned (a power reserved to the states and their subdivisions) in such a way as to prevent their subdivision. The subdividers then had no further use for the property, withdrew their bids, and the GSA had to allow the state to take possession, under federal law which gives the states and localities certain special rights to acquire otherwise unsold surplus federal lands within their boundaries.[6]

In some cases, the states use their powers to advance clearly national interests. During the late 1950's, when the testing of nuclear weapons in the atmosphere was raising levels of radiation to ever new peaks, to the dismay of many scientists and medical experts, the federal Atomic Energy Commission repeatedly ignored any efforts on the part of the public to ascertain the exact

[6] This incident is described in Nelson A. Rockefeller, *The Future of Federalism* (Cambridge, Mass.: Harvard University Press, 1962).

amounts of radioactive fallout and contamination reaching the American people. At that point, several of the states, on their own initiative, through their own legislation and the activities of their own public health departments, began collecting samples of the atmosphere, the soil, and their local crops, tested them, and made their findings public. These states not only publicized their findings (the Minnesota Health Department published daily reports of the radiation count), thus influencing public opinion with telling results, but in some cases began to take steps to control potential sources of public contamination within their purview.[7]

The states could do this despite AEC recalcitrance and even in the face of AEC opposition because they had independent agencies with independent sources of power. Even though these agencies used federal funds for some of their other activities, in the last analysis they remained beholden to their states. And even though their officials undoubtedly saw eye to eye with their federal counterparts on most matters, they could take public issue with a federal agency with impunity when they felt it necessary to do so.

In general, cases of either sort of conflict are rare since functional sharing among governments usually reflects something close to a general consensus on policy matters on the part of the general public and the specialized "publics" at all levels of government. Still, the possibilities for independent action remain real ones.

[7] See William H. Berman and Lee M. Hydeman, *Federal and State Responsibilities for Radiation Protection: The Need for Federal Legislation* (Ann Arbor: University of Michigan Law School, 1959) for a review of state activities and federal-state relations in the atomic energy field until the enactment of the 1959 amendments to the Atomic Energy Act of 1954. The history of atomic energy regulation is an excellent example of the way in which programs initiated unilaterally by the federal government are decentralized to fit into the cooperative system because of the preexisting demands of American federalism. The formal devolution of federal regulatory functions to the states (to supplement those already exercised by the states under their general police powers) has been going on since 1959, with increasing momentum.

Theodore Lownik Library
Illinois Benedictine College
Lisle, Illinois 60532

Financing the Partnership

Part of the reason for the development of this kind of sharing as a means to maintain the position of the states and their localities lies in the very real, if not explicit, supremacy of the federal government in matters of taxing and spending. Though the power to tax and spend is constitutionally concurrent, the federal government has been in a better position to use its share of the power over the years, for constitutional and political reasons. This position, strong in 1790, was further strengthened by the adoption of the federal income tax amendment in 1913 (Figure 2). Rather

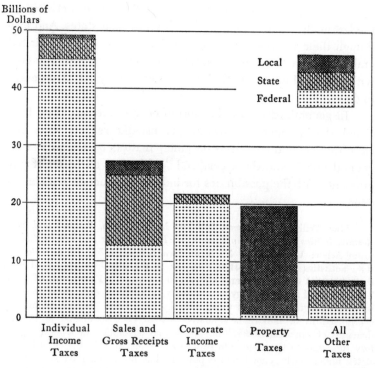

FIGURE 2. Tax Revenues by Type of Tax and Level of Government, 1962

than resist this trend, which is reenforced by so many factors, the states and localities have developed means to capitalize on it in a manner calculated to maximize their ability to control the expenditure of funds passing through their hands, no matter what their source. The states have actually used such funds to extend their control over their own local subdivisions by exercising the federal requirements attached to the funds as a device to expand their own supervisory responsibilities.

Political pressures generated in the states and localities to gain federal financial assistance for governmental services, coupled with an increasing interest in those services on the part of federal officials (particularly professionals in the various functional fields), have led to the development of an elaborate system of federal transfers of payments to the states and localities for a wide variety of activities. Since the early nineteenth century, it has been clear that Congress may use its taxing (and other revenue-raising) powers to support federal-state cooperative programs, attaching such conditions to its grants as it deems proper and providing for the withholding or revocation of such grants as it deems necessary.

The twentieth century has unquestionably witnessed a great expansion of federal expenditures. At least in the realm of cash outlays, the federal share of total government expenditures has increased from 34.5 per cent in 1902 to 64.3 per cent in 1962. Yet

Table 8. Relative Federal and State-Local Expenditures, 1948 and 1960

	ALL FUNCTIONS	DEFENSE CONNECTED FUNCTIONS	CIVIL FUNCTIONS
1948			
Federal	65	97	39
State-Local	35	3	61
1960			
Federal	60	99.8	30
State-Local	40	0.2	70

SOURCE: U.S. Bureau of the Census.

this gross sum is misleading. Until World War II, total state and local expenditures combined still exceeded the total federal expenditures. Since 1945, when the war-inflated federal share reached over 90 per cent of the total, the proportions have been narrowing to the point where state and local expenditures are presently approaching 40 per cent of all government outlays (or 70 per cent of the total federal outlay), including those for defense. Despite the heavy burdens of defense spending which have fallen on the federal government since 1950, the trend has been to increase the state-local share of governmental expenditure in the United States. Compare, for example, relative percentages of federal and state-local expenditures for 1948 and 1960 (Table 8).

The central fiscal role of the states and their local subdivisions is even more pronounced when government expenditures for *domestic* purposes only are considered. In the domestic realm, state-local expenditures are still far greater than those of the federal government, accounting for over 60 per cent of the total, much as in the past. Between 1956 and 1960, over 70 per cent of the total federal expenditure was for national defense or defense-related activities. In the past thirty years federal expenditures for domestic functions, expressed as a percentage of the gross national product, have *decreased* while state-local expenditures have remained nearly constant by the same measure. The raw figures provided in Table 9 lend themselves to these and other comparisons of similar import.

The magnitude of this change is best revealed by looking at the expenditures of the individual states. The present annual state government expenditures of New York and California, the nation's two largest states, exceed $5 billion, with over $8 billion spent by each state and its local subdivisions combined, far more than the average annual federal budget for the years preceding World War II. In 1963, nine states had annual budgets exceeding $1 billion, *excluding* local expenditures which generally doubled the total in each. Combined state-local expenditures exceeded $1 billion annually in at least twenty-two states and $3 billion in five.

Table 9. Federal, State, and Local Finances, 1938–1963 (in millions of dollars)

	TOTAL EXPENDITURES a			TOTAL REVENUES a		STATE AND LOCAL REVENUES FROM FEDERAL GOVERNMENT		OUTSTANDING DEBT	
	FEDERAL TOTAL	FEDERAL CIVIL FUNCTIONS b	STATE AND LOCAL	FEDERAL	STATE AND LOCAL	TOTAL	PER CENT	FEDERAL	STATE AND LOCAL
1938	8,449	5,978	9,988	7,226	11,058	800	7.2	37,165	19,436
1942	35,549	7,488	10,914	16,062	13,148	858	6.5	72,422	19,706
1946	66,534	9,674	14,067	46,405	15,983	855	5.3	269,422	15,917
1950	44,800	19,245	27,905	43,527	25,639	2,486	9.7	257,357	24,115
1954	77,692	20,820	36,607	75,835	35,386	2,966	8.4	271,260	38,931
1956	75,991	24,903	43,152	81,294	41,692	3,335	8.0	272,751	48,868
1958	86,054	30,267	53,712	86,006	49,262	4,865	9.9	276,343	58,187
1960	97,284	38,074	60,999	99,800	60,277	6,974	11.6	286,331	69,955
1961	104,863	43,291	67,023	101,341	64,531	7,131	11.1	288,971	75,023
1962	113,428	47,670	70,547	106,441	69,492	7,871	11.3	298,201	81,278
1963 c	118,805	50,046	75,760	114,557	75,317	8,722	11.6	305,860	87,451

a Totals include trust funds, sales revenues, etc., and reflect a more accurate picture of government activity than general revenue and expenditure figures alone.

b Excludes expenditures for defense, foreign relations, space, some veterans' services, and interest on the general debt (which was created primarily by defense spending).

c Preliminary figures.

SOURCES: Advisory Commission on Intergovernmental Relations and Congressional Quarterly.

[65]

Nor is this growth in state and local expenditures simply a reflection of increased transfers of federal funds. Despite the increase in federal transfers of payments to the states and their local subdivisions in recent years, and the general increase in federal spending for domestic programs since 1932, state and local expenditures based on their own revenues have been increasing with great rapidity. This is reflected in the relatively low proportions of federal as against state-local expenditures for specific programs. In 1962, the federal government granted the states and localities $1,169 billion for education programs, or no more than 5.3 per cent of the total state and local general expenditure for education.[8] That same year, the federal government granted the states and localities $2,748 billion for highway construction, a

Table 10. *Direct Domestic Expenditures of the Three Levels of Government, Selected Functions, 1961* (in millions of dollars)

FUNCTION	FEDERAL	TOTAL, STATE-LOCAL	STATE	LOCAL
Education	640	*20,382*	3,792	16,590
Highways	151	*9,785*	6,230	330
Public Welfare	59	*4,673*	2,311	2,362
Hospitals	1,053	*3,425*	1,799	1,626
Health	542	590	260	3,555
Police	193	*1,991*	261	1,730
Agriculture & Natural Resources	*10,082*	1,327	906	421
Housing & Urban Renewal	377	*943*	7	936
Air & Water Transportation	*2,358*	715	114	601
Social Insurance Administration	285	*351*	351	—

NOTE: Italicized figures indicate the major share of total governmental expenditure for a function.

SOURCE: U.S. Department of Commerce.

[8] With the enactment of the "Great Society" education measures, this figure has better than doubled but remains a relatively minor though growing source of school funds.

major cooperative program but still only 26.5 per cent of their total general expenditures for that purpose. Even in the realm of housing and urban renewal, where the federal stimulus is most important, the 1962 federal grant of $352 million provided only 30.5 per cent of the state-local general expenditure in that field. If certain earmarked revenues omitted for bookkeeping reasons were added to the state-local column, the federal percentage would in almost every case be even lower.

When the actual expenditure of funds is considered, after the transfer of funds among governments has been completed, the role of the states and their subdivisions is enhanced even further, as shown in Table 10. Even where federal funds are involved, the federal government undertakes few operational responsibilities.

State and local payrolls are increasing apace. In October 1952, state government payrolls alone amounted to $271 million per month. Ten years later, the unadjusted figure had better than doubled to reach $635 million monthly. Of the 9,404,000 persons on public payrolls in 1962, some 1,682,000 (18 per cent) were state employees and some 5,187,000 (58 per cent) were local employees for a state-local total of 6,869,000 or 76 per cent of the total public employment.

The Forms of Sharing [9]

Though the most characteristic device used to promote sharing among governments is the cash grant-in-aid (federal-state, state-local, or federal-local), cooperation is actually promoted through several devices. Among the most common are those of *informal cooperation*—through conferences, the provision of advisory and training services, the exchange of general services, the lending of equipment and personnel, and the performance of services by one

[9] This section is based in part on material prepared for the author's article, "The Shaping of Intergovernmental Relations in the Twentieth Century," in *The Annals of the American Academy of Political and Social Science* (May 1965), pp. 10–22. See also Jane Perry Clark, *The Rise of a New Federalism* (New York: Columbia University Press, 1938).

government in place of another. Such collaboration is barely visible to the general public except when a conference is sponsored by the White House or when a public health team moves in on the heels of an epidemic. The informal luncheon meeting or the use of local fire-fighting equipment on a nearby airbase attract virtually no attention whatsoever even though they may represent continuing programs of great importance.

Formal cooperative activities, on the other hand, are based on *contracts and compacts for cooperative action*. In the largest sense, contractual relationships are basic to a federal system which is founded upon a fundamental compact to begin with. In essence, it is the contractual relationship that makes possible large-scale intergovernmental cooperation to achieve common ends. Every formal cooperative relationship involves some form of contractual tie. The flexibility of the contract as a device enhances its usefulness and allows it to be used for many purposes. There are contractual relationships for cooperative research, for the division of costs to support shared activities, for provision of exchange of services, for prevention of conflict or misunderstanding, for exchange of personnel, for joint enforcement of laws, for sharing revenues, and for lending agreements.

Recurring informal contacts are often formalized to the point of receiving statutory recognition and contractual ratification through *contracts for operational sharing*. These are relationships that involve nothing more than a formal agreement to share resources or tasks without formal transfers of funds or personnel from one government to another. They are often used to prevent needless duplication of time, money, and effort or to enhance the possibilities for more comprehensive execution of particular programs. State-federal crop reports, Bureau of Labor Statistics calculations, administration of the selective service system, state regulation of nuclear installations, and formal agreements for the exchange of tax information or cooperative inspections of public utilities are examples of this type of relationship.

Another form of cooperation involves the *interchange of personnel*. This includes the provision of "services-in-aid," i.e., arrangements by one government to lend its personnel to assist another, jointly paid agents, and the deputization of personnel of one government by another. Under this type of cooperative activity, federal engineers are lent to states and localities to plan projects; county agricultural agents are paid with federal, state, and local funds and have special obligations to all three governments; and state hospital guards are deputized by the local police.

The pervasiveness of the partnership has led to the development of *interdependent activities* in which one government depends upon another (or both depend on each other) for the enforcement of laws or the administration of programs otherwise not apparently shared. The administration of elections is one good example of this. The election of national officials is contingent upon state implementation of the constitutional requirements. In this case, there is federal dependence upon state action. States, on the other hand, may depend upon federal authorities to exclude the transportation of goods prohibited by state law (liquor, oleomargarine, firecrackers) across their boundaries.

As mentioned previously, first in importance among the forms of intergovernmental cooperation are the *grants-in-aid,* federal transfers of funds to the states and federal or state transfers to local governments for specified purposes usually subject to a measure of supervision and review by the granting government. They are particularly distinctive because they involve the transfer of funds from one government to another to attain certain agreed-upon ends. The first grants-in-aid were generally transfers of land to the recipient governments to be sold to finance specific programs. Fifteen such grant-in-land programs were established by the federal government in the nineteenth century. Supervision of these grants was relatively loose but still significant. The relatively few conditions attached to them governed the mode of disposition of the lands and the manner in which the proceeds were to be used for the purposes specified.

Cash grants-in-aid also date from the nineteenth century (six were established before 1900) but did not flower until the twentieth. Since 1911 some sixty-five new federal grant-in-aid programs have been established, fourteen of which have since been discontinued. In general, they have been rigorously administered by all governments concerned, in great measure because of the more stringent conditions attached to them than to the grants-in-land.

Grants-in-aid are of three kinds. Flat grants provide each recipient government with an equal sum regardless of local conditions or deviations from the national mean. They generally do not require formal matching of funds by the recipient governments, though they may require the recipients to shoulder administrative costs. Most of the land grants were of this type, as are state per capita grants to local school districts. Proportionate grants are those made to recipient governments in proportion to their own contributions to the program or project in question. They are often allocated on the basis of formulas which take the needs and capabilities of the recipient into account. Federal highway and education grants are of this type. Percentage grants are allocated like proportionate grants, but the granter's contribution is fixed as a set percentage of the cost to the grantee for maintaining a particular program. Among the best known are the federal public welfare grants and some state grants to local school districts. Grants-in-aid may also include grants-in-kind: timber from the public lands, surplus commodities and property, obsolete military equipment, or the like. These generally resemble flat grants and are rarely subject to extensive supervision.

Other forms of intergovernmental sharing include *tax offsets* (used when nationwide compliance is necessary, as in the unemployment compensation program), *shared revenues* (such as timber and mineral royalties and shared license fees), and *grants or contracts awarded on similar terms to public and private applicants* (such as federal grants to universities). These all represent variations of the grant-in-aid principle, developed to meet conditions which would frustrate simpler grant mechanisms. Each of these devices has a long history extending back to the nineteenth century at the very least, and each has been sanctioned through different modes of constitutional interpretation.

Furthermore, each has its own "politics," a variation on the overall theme of the partnership.

Perhaps the most outstanding characteristic of the federal grants and shared revenues in the context of internal state politics is that the political struggle over the use and distribution of the money is essentially an intrastate matter. In practically all the major programs channeled through the states, the federal funds are so mixed in with state funds after their transfer that the local beneficiaries have no idea whose money they are receiving. Their efforts to obtain funds are essentially directed toward the state house, not toward the national capitol.[10]

There are three exceptions to this rule. Occasionally the localities must struggle with the state legislature to gain state participation in a federal program that might benefit them or to obtain state authorization for them to participate if it is a direct federal-local program (as in the case of urban renewal). Such conflicts are particularly frequent in previously rural states in the process of urbanizing. The rural interests, endeavoring to hang onto a passing era, resist virtually all demands of the state's burgeoning cities. Such was the case in Iowa until 1961. Before then, the rural-oriented legislature refused to allow the state's cities to participate in federal aid urban renewal programs, so that even though the federal aid was directed to the localities, they could not accept it.[11]

In some federal-state programs, particularly the smaller ones, the amount of federal funds allocated to each state by Congress is much less than is needed to satisfy local demands.[12] Local com-

[10] This is true in the twenty-five states studied in Governmental Affairs Institute, *A Survey Report on the Impact of Federal Grants-in-Aid on the Structure and Functions of State and Local Governments,* submitted to the Commission on Intergovernmental Relations (Washington: Government Printing Office, 1956). The writer has confirmed the same in three additional States (Georgia, Minnesota, and Wisconsin) through field research. Of course this is not true of the direct federal-local grants.

[11] Field research, Davenport and Des Moines, Iowa, 1960, and *General Laws of Iowa,* 1961.

[12] Congress makes it a practice to apportion federal expenditures among the states wherever technically possible as a means of insuring maximum

munities then enter into competition at the state level to gain a share of the allocated funds for their own projects. While this competition is essentially intrastate in character, it may be conducted at the federal level when the issue involves the congressional division of state allocations in federal-local programs. In any case, it is initiated for specific federal-aided projects known to the localities. In certain situations, the localities can even call upon federal personnel stationed within them to assist them in advancing their claims.[13]

Finally, in recent years the "pilot project" has become a new way for local communities to get additional federal aid. In many of these cases, the localities must compete with other local communities in Washington for special grants. Usually they are supported by legislative and administrative representatives of their states but the burden of the struggle remains on their shoulders.

Direct Federal Expenditures

The greatest impact of federal spending within the United States comes, not from transfers of payments to state or local governments, but from defense-related expenditures and direct payments to private individuals, primarily farmers, veterans, and pensioners and increasingly to college students. Direct payments, including government grants to institutions for civilian research, average out to approximately three times the total amount transferred to

---

nationwide participation in federal or federal aid programs and to encourage even the weaker and smaller states to participate in them. The manner in which the apportionment is made varies from program to program but the system includes ostensibly unilateral federal programs as well as the various programs involving intergovernmental transfers of payments. For details on the intergovernmental transfers, see Advisory Commission on Intergovernmental Relations, *The Role of Equalization in Federal Grants* (January 1964).

[13] The writer has evidence of extensive use of federal personnel stationed locally to lobby for community development projects requiring federal aid in Arkansas, Georgia, Illinois, Wisconsin, and Colorado from his field work in those states in 1958, 1960, 1961, and 1962. Evidence of this in other states is available in the files of the Workshop in American Federalism (formerly of the University of Chicago), Temple University.

the states through federal grants each year. Defense contracts represent the great bulk of the direct federal expenditures within the states. In fiscal 1962 alone, new contracts worth $27,800,400,000 were awarded, approximately four times the total amount distributed through federal grants that same year.[14]

When the state-by-state distribution of federal defense contract expenditures is considered, it is apparent that the old adage "Them that has, gets" applies. Those states "tooled up" for defense production are repeatedly favored. This is not just a matter of objective efficiency. Part of the "having" is having well-developed methods for influencing the allocation of contracts. Here is where it again becomes obvious that the states function as civil societies or, to put it more directly, that the successful states do. Local industries seeking contracts and local communities seeking defense installations work closely with state congressional delegations and state and local political officials lobbying in Washington. In some cases, states and the larger cities have established Washington offices, virtually embassies, to work with their congressional delegations. Massachusetts has been particularly active in this regard for two decades, its Washington office having been opened in 1941. The gains registered by that state since 1961 were not simply a matter of having a Kennedy in the White House but represented the fruition of hard work by the state's "man in Washington," beginning in 1956 when Governor Foster Furcolo reorganized the office and formalized its relationships with the Massachusetts congressional delegation.[15]

In fact, states in different sections of the country are favored differently by different kinds of federal aid. Just to cite some examples, southern and smaller western states are favored with a higher per capita return of federal grant funds as part of the ostensibly equalizing aspects of federal grant-in-aid programs.

[14] Tax Foundation, *Facts and Figures on Government Finance, 1962–1963*, 12th ed. (Englewood Cliffs, N.J.: Prentice-Hall, 1963).

[15] Meeting with Lewis A. Dexter (formerly affiliated with Governor Furcolo on this project), September 9, 1957. Kennedy, in fact, was not really interested in performing this kind of service for his state.

Southern states have been favored with military installations since the Spanish-American War. Their state leaders, from congressmen to chambers of commerce, have become especially adept at securing and maintaining such installations. The states of the Southwest and Far West have been particularly successful in gaining military procurement contracts which have led to the creation of whole new industries and which, in turn, have enabled those states to develop, maintain, and enlarge their "boom" economies.[16] They have been particularly successful in acquiring a virtual monopoly over the nation's aerospace programs, offering climate as an inducement to those interested in year-round testing operations and year-round "outdoor living." The New England states have had a measure of success in attracting federal funds for research and development by capitalizing on their already excellent research and educational facilities and by developing channels of influence in Washington. There is some indication that the northern tier of states dominated by the moralistic political culture (see Chapter Four) and the larger states having greater professional expertise to draw upon acquire a high percentage of the pilot project grants because they have people in key positions interested in experimentation and supported in their efforts by their publics. In recent years, federal officials have made a conscious effort to favor states with major depressed areas in the distribution of all kinds of federal projects.

In all the foregoing cases, the key to the acquisition of federal benefits is intensive state and local activity to secure those benefits. The better a state is able to function as a coordinated civil society, the more likely it is to obtain a large share of federal expenditures to stimulate its economy. California and Texas—

[16] There is some evidence that defense contracts given the Henry J. Kaiser industries and others in California during World War II were of first importance in providing the West with an industrial base able to compete successfully with northeastern-owned industries for the first time. As the West Coast industries began to develop their own capital pools, they were able to take steps to eliminate the eastern "colonialism" that had burdened their section before the war and thus to change the economic structure of the country.

both virtually self-governing commonwealths in many ways, with strong traditions of intrastate cohesiveness vis-à-vis the outside world—stand as the most successful examples of the truth of this rule. The failure of Michigan—a state torn by internal dissension approaching class conflict for many years—to maintain its position in the competition for federal contracts in the years following the Korean War confirms its validity. Internal conflicts prevented Michigan, the "arsenal of democracy" in World War II, from helping its industry adjust to changing military procurement needs and consequently lost the state its position as a major center of defense production. More recently, Michigan's leaders have recognized the necessity for the people of that state to develop a common spirit in order to maintain a viable local economy and have been fostering state consciousness in a number of ways with increasing success.[17] Pennsylvania's recent experience, on the other hand, indicates how by learning to function as a more cohesive civil society, a state can do much to gain federal aid to improve its depressed economy.

The two kinds of federal transfers of payments serve to divide the political contest over funds into two parts—the intrastate struggle for grant funds to be used for public services and the interstate struggle for federal contracts and direct expenditures. It appears that there is little interstate struggle for the public service dollar outside Congress. By now Washington has the formula system down pat and all that must be done is to arrive at an agreement on what kind of formula to use when new programs are inaugurated or old ones revised. Since it has become clear that the margin of allowable gain within the formula structure is limited and the representatives of the states generally recognize the virtues of some measure of redistribution of the national wealth through federal grants, Congress expends relatively little effort in fighting over it. By the same token, there is little intrastate conflict over defense funds. This is not only because defense funds repre-

---

[17] This recognition is documented in William Haber, Eugene C. McKean, and Harold C. Taylor, *What's Ahead for Michigan* (Kalamazoo: The W. E. Upjohn Institute, 1959).

sent direct federal expenditures which do not pass through state hands. Within the successful states there is a gentleman's agreement that, while localities or locally based industries are free to submit their own bids up to a point, once the federal authorities have indicated any preferences, the entire state will concentrate its efforts on behalf of its favored community.

Direct Federal-Local Relations

Of rising importance in the overall scheme of intergovernmental relations and of extreme importance in the matter of preserving the states' integrity is the question of direct federal aid to localities. Contrary to the general impression, the federal government has been supplying direct aid to local communities since the early nineteenth century, then, as now, primarily in the field of internal improvements and secondarily in the field of education. In recent years, however, great metropolitan centers have emerged which face problems of urban reconstruction—both physical and social —of an unprecedented magnitude. These great cities, virtually civil societies in their own right, are politically able to make their influence felt in Washington and are organizationally strong enough to handle the complexities of administering cooperative programs. They have been active in securing the right to develop direct city-federal relationships in certain aspects of the airport construction, urban renewal, and housing fields. Even in these cases, however, the states retain the right to involve themselves in the relationship if they choose to do so.

Most recently, federal and big city authorities have sought to establish direct federal-local ties to implement aspects of the new antipoverty, economic development, and education programs. This trend is partly a reflection of new attitudes in Washington, partly an effort to bypass those state governments in the South hostile to the civil rights aspects of those programs, and partly an attempt to break through established power structures to reach certain excluded groups. In the antipoverty programs there is a tendency to bypass not only the states but also local governments in an effort to bring in public nongovernmental welfare groups and the poor themselves.

While the effect of these new tendencies cannot be assessed as yet, what is clear is that the weight of constitutional tradition is operating to give central roles in the implementation of even the most direct new federal-local programs to those energetic state governments wishing to keep command of developments within their jurisdictions. The antipoverty program, for example, is designed to provide federal money directly for locally sponsored projects, but as enacted by Congress, the state governors have some measure of veto power over most projects proposed within the limits of their states. In fact, most of the first antipoverty grants in 1964 were made either to state agencies or to previously constituted local bodies operating in cooperation with state agencies. Moreover, many states have established or designated state-level coordinating bodies to bring order out of the potential chaos of local public and private bodies competing for federal funds, thus rendering one of the traditional services of the state governments in the federal system. As usual, those states that are energetically engaged in developing their own antipoverty programs or are cleverly adapting existing programs to the "antipoverty" idea are best able to secure substantial control over any of the "federal" activities within their borders.

CHAPTER FOUR

The States and the Political Setting

The Cooperative System and the Political Setting

While the practice of cooperative federalism is nationwide, the fifty states respond to the cooperative system in different ways. Understanding their responses requires an appreciation of two sets of relationships: (1) the way in which the states functioning as political systems influence the operations of the general government and (2) the way in which the states—still functioning as political systems—adapt national programs to their own needs and interests. To appreciate those relationships, it is first necessary to understand the fundamental social and political factors which serve to shape them and the political setting in which they operate.

Because the states function to divide a nationwide socioeconomic system along territorial lines, the primary socio-economic influences on their political systems are those which are most clearly expressed through territorial manifestations. In this light, three overarching factors appear to be especially important in shaping the individual states' political structures, electoral behavior, and modes of organization for political action. They are *political culture*—the particular pattern of orientation to political action in which each political system is imbedded; *sectionalism*— the more or less permanent arrangements that tie groups of contiguous states or segments of states together with bonds of shared economic and social interests; and the continuing *frontier*—the constant effort of Americans to progressively extend their control over the natural environment for man's benefit and the consequent periodic reorganization of American social and settlement patterns as a result of the impact of that effort. All three of these factors represent dynamic processes rather than static situations which act upon the states and the federal system generally and interact with each other in ever-changing ways. Between them, the three factors embrace and shape the primary social, economic, and psychological thrusts that influence American politics, while other factors often considered basic to the shaping of political systems, ranging from the class system to urbanization, are embraced within them and are secondary in their influence.

Political culture is particularly important as the historical source of such differences in habits, concerns, and attitudes that exist to influence political life in the various states. Sectionalism is particularly important as a major source of geographical variations that influence state by state differences in responding to nationwide political, economic, and social developments. The frontier is particularly important as the generator of the forces of change that influence patterns of settlement and economic organization throughout the federal system; that stimulate governmental action in new fields at all levels; and that consequently force the continual readjustment of the federal balance.

In this chapter and Chapter Five we will be concerned with these three factors as dynamic processes affecting the states through their particular pattern of interaction in each. An attempt will be made to (1) outline the particular characteristics of political culture and sectionalism in the United States and the relationship of both to the continuing frontier, (2) relate all three to the varying responses of the states to the cooperative system, and (3) suggest ways in which the three factors influence the states as political systems.[1]

[1] The ideas presented in this and the following chapter should be considered in the nature of hypotheses rooted in an effort to organize the complex phenomena that shape American civilization and its politics so as to enhance our understanding of both. As the elements in an overarching hypothesis, the three factors can best be understood through a combination of qualitative analysis and quantitative measurement. Relatively little quantitative data is available since there has yet to be sufficient research into the character and influence of the three factors either on a national basis or in

Federalism and Political Culture

One of the observations coming out of the several studies of federal-state relations conducted in the 1950's was that the states themselves (or their local subdivisions) could virtually dictate the impact of federal-aided activities within their boundaries.[2] Take the case of the impact of federal aid on the administration of state government. In those states where administration is concentrated at the executive level and the governor is usually strong, federal aid has tended to strengthen executive powers by giving the governor more and better tools to wield.[3] In those states where power is widely diffused among the separate executive departments, federal aid has tended to add to the diffusion by giving the individual departments new sources of funds outside of the normal channels of state control which can even be used to obtain more money and power from the legislature. In those states where earmarked funds reflect legislature or lobby domination over programs, earmarked federal funds have had the same effect. Despite many protestations to the contrary, only in rare situations have federal grant programs served to alter state administrative patterns in ways that did not coincide with already established state policies, though such grants have often sharpened certain tendencies in state administration.

---

specific states. What is known, however, provides a useful basis for comparing state politics in our federal system. The data used here represent the substance of the author's research as delineated in another connection in footnote 7 of Chapter One. Space limitations make it necessary to concentrate on only a few aspects of these factors to indicate something of their character and influence. A full display of the data available from that research must await publication of a work devoted to this question alone.

[2] Governmental Affairs Institute, *A Survey Report on the Impact of Federal Grants-in-Aid on the Structure and Functions of State and Local Governments,* submitted to the Commission on Intergovernmental Relations (Washington: Government Printing Office, 1956). The statements in this and the following paragraphs are based in large part on the findings in the twenty-five states covered in that report.

[3] For a study of this problem in one state, see *The Office of Governor* (Urbana: Institute of Government and Public Affairs, University of Illinois, 1963).

Or, in the case of federal merit system requirements, states dominated by political attitudes conducive to notions of professionalization and the isolation of certain forms of government activity from the pressures of partisan politics have had little problem adjusting their programs to meet federal standards, since they had either adopted similar standards earlier or were quite in sympathy with the standards when proposed. Minnesota, for example, has tighter merit system requirements than those applicable to its federal-aided programs under the Hatch Act. On the other hand, states dominated by a political outlook that has little sympathy for nonpartisanship in government administration (Kentucky and West Virginia, for example) have had a more difficult time adjusting to federal requirements of this sort and have often worked to find ways to circumvent them, even while conforming to them superficially. States with a similar lack of interest in civil service reform whose environment is also shaped by advanced industrial and commercial organization are generally open to the organizational aspects of the federal requirements if only because their dominant economic organizations already reflect the modern organizational approach. So, even if the dominant political interests in states like Massachusetts, Pennsylvania, or Illinois object to the *political* aspects of Hatch Act requirements, they are in reasonable harmony with their *organizational* demands.[4]

A parallel situation exists in regard to the substance of the federal programs. Every state has certain dominant traditions about what constitutes proper government action and every state

[4] The merit system example has the additional advantage of revealing some of the complexities encountered in this kind of analysis. While the overt state by state differences are relatively clear-cut, significant nuances of complexity just below the surface make the role of the three overarching factors more pronounced. Thus, willingness to embrace merit systems is not to be equated with opposition to patronage systems, per se. For example, the same state can actually maintain both if its public does not associate patronage with political corruption but rather with Jacksonian ideas of democratic access to government offices. In some states, the concept "political employee" immediately conjures up the image of the less than honest party hack or of a shiftless relative of an elected officeholder. In those states, the introduction of "nonpolitical" merit standards is placed in juxtaposition to the patronage system and is considered a revolutionary change in that it supposedly sepa-

is generally predisposed toward those federal programs it can accept as consistent with those traditions. Many states have pioneered programs that fit into their traditions before the initiation of similar ones at the federal level or on a nationwide basis through federal aid. This, too, tends to lessen the impact of federal action on the political systems of those states and also to lessen any negative state reaction to federal entrance into particular fields. Wisconsin's pioneering efforts in social welfare before the New Deal are well known. They became the models for many of the new federal-aid programs which were often drawn so as to minimize the dislocation to that state's established programs. The majority of Minnesota's congressional delegation is continually at the forefront in supporting new federal-aid welfare and internal improvement programs because as a state, Minnesota is predisposed toward positive government action and finds such programs useful in supporting its own goals. Today states like California accept federal aid for mental health programs not as an innovative device but as a reenforcement of existing programs. Professional mental health workers in states like New Jersey rely upon the same federal grants to keep their programs free of internally generated political pressures, arguing with the patronage-inclined legislatures that federal regulations demand that professional standards be maintained. Their colleagues in states like Illinois use federal aid to force the hands of their legislatures to expand state activities in new directions. Reformers interested in mental health in states like Mississippi are interested in federal aid to inaugurate new programs. In matters of national defense, the southern states have a long tradition of supporting state militia and National Guard units

rates "politics" from "administration." In some states, however, the patronage appointee is not considered dishonest or somehow deficient *a priori*, and political appointment is recognized as a possible source of good officeholders. In those states merit systems are often introduced in response to a temporary lapse from the accepted public standards of public employment by the political organization in power which has led to a public reaction against the method of appointment or, perhaps even more often, they are advanced as a means to raise professional standards in certain branches of the state service where professionalism is considered desirable. For still other variations in the subsurface meaning of civil service reform, see Chapter Five.

so that over the years they have taken greater advantage of federal subventions for the maintenance of military reserve units than most of their sisters have.[5]

Many of these and other differences in state responses within the federal system appear to be stimulated by differences in political culture among the states. We have already defined political culture as the particular pattern of orientation to political action in which each political system is imbedded. Political culture, like all culture, is rooted in the cumulative historical experiences of particular groups of people. Indeed, the origins of particular patterns of political culture are often lost in the mists of time. Patterns of political culture frequently overlap several political systems, and two or more political cultures may coexist within the same political system.[6] Though little is known about the precise ways in which political culture is influential, it is possible to suggest some ways in which the differences in political culture are likely to be significant.

Three aspects of political culture stand out as particularly influential in shaping the operations of the state political systems within the context of American federalism. They are (1) the set of perceptions of what politics is and what can be expected from government, held by both the general public and the politicians;

---

[5] Gross state by state variations in political behavior and program support in several important fields are chronicled within a comparative framework in Herbert Jacob and Kenneth N. Vines, eds., *Politics in the American States* (Boston: Little, Brown, 1965), an excellent source for comparing the states as political systems.

[6] For a more complete definition of political culture, see Gabriel A. Almond, "Comparative Political Systems," *The Journal of Politics*, XVIII (1956), 391–409. Political culture is directly connected to historical phenomena. Specific elements of political culture frequently have their origins in historical events or situations which cause great and long-lasting changes among those who share the experiences they generate. These changes are then transmitted—and often intensified—through the process of acculturation to the descendants of the original group, including both "blood" and "galvanized" (those adopted into the group) descendants. Perhaps because of the close relationship between political culture and historical phenomena, historians have done more to trace the ingredients that combine to create the patterns of political culture than have other social scientists. Though they have not done so to investigate political culture as such, they have provided

(2) the kinds of people who become active in government and politics, as holders of elective offices, members of the bureaucracy, and active political workers; and (3) the actual way in which the art of government is practiced by citizens, politicians, and public officials in the light of their perceptions. In turn, the cultural components of individual and group behavior in the various political systems make themselves felt at three levels: in the kind of civic behavior dictated by conscience and internalized ethical standards; in the character of law-abidingness displayed by citizens and officials; and in the positive actions of government.

Marketplace and Commonwealth and the Three Political Cultures

The United States as a whole shares a general political culture.[7] This American political culture is rooted in two contrasting conceptions of American political order, both of which can be traced back to the earliest settlement of the country. In the first, the political order is conceived as a marketplace in which the primary public relationships are products of bargaining among individuals and groups acting out of self-interest. In the second, the political order is conceived to be a commonwealth—a state in which the whole people have an undivided interest—in which the citizens cooperate in an effort to create and maintain the best government

---

the raw materials for such an investigation through their studies of other phenomena, such as migration patterns, political alliances and antagonisms, the historical roots of continuing social behavior, and the like. This chapter draws heavily on their work in both acknowledged and unacknowleged ways.

Since the study of political culture is still in its infancy, the discussion of the American political subcultures in this chapter should be considered a preliminary one, no more. It should raise more questions than it answers. At the same time, the writer firmly believes that the outline set down here will stand up under the scrutiny of future studies even as specific elements within it may be altered by further research findings.

[7] For an analysis by political scientists of the national political culture in a comparative setting, see Gabriel A. Almond and Sidney Verba, *The Civic Culture* (Princeton: Princeton University Press, 1963).

in order to implement certain shared moral principles. These two conceptions have exercised an influence on government and politics throughout American history, sometimes in conflict and sometimes by complementing one another.

The national political culture is itself a synthesis of three major political subcultures which jointly inhabit the country, existing side by side or even overlapping one another. All three are of nationwide proportions, having spread, in the course of time, from coast to coast. At the same time each subculture is strongly tied to specific sections of the country, reflecting the currents of migration that have carried people of different origins and backgrounds across the continent in more or less orderly patterns.

Considering the central characteristics that govern each and their respective centers of emphasis, the three political cultures may be called individualistic (I), moralistic (M), and traditionalistic (T).[8] Each of the three reflects its own particular synthesis of the marketplace and the commonwealth.

The Individualistic Political Culture

The *individualistic political culture* emphasizes the conception of the democratic order as a marketplace. In its view, a government is instituted for strictly utilitarian reasons, to handle those functions demanded by the people it is created to serve. A government need not have any direct concern with questions of the "good society" except insofar as it may be used to advance some common conception of the good society formulated outside the political arena just as it serves other functions. Since the individualistic political culture emphasizes the centrality of private concerns, it places a premium on limiting community intervention—whether governmental or nongovernmental—into private activi-

[8] The names given the three political subcultures are meant to be descriptive, not evaluative. By the same token, the descriptions of the three that follow are intended to be models or ideal types not fully extant in the real world.

ties to the minimum necessary to keep the marketplace in proper working order. In general, government action is to be restricted to those areas, primarily in the economic realm, which encourage private initiative and widespread access to the marketplace.[9]

The character of political participation in systems dominated by the individualistic political culture reflects this outlook. The individualistic political culture holds politics to be just another means by which individuals may improve themselves socially and economically. In this sense politics is a "business" like any other that competes for talent and offers rewards to those who take it up as a career. Those individuals who choose political careers may rise by providing the governmental services demanded of them and, in return, may expect to be adequately compensated for their efforts. Interpretations of officeholders' obligations under this arrangement vary among political systems and even among individuals within a single political system. Where the norms are high, such people are expected to provide high quality government services for the general public in the best possible manner in return for the status and economic rewards considered their due. Some who choose political careers clearly commit themselves to such norms; others believe that an officeholder's primary responsibility is to serve himself and those who have supported him

[9] It is important to examine this description and the ones following it very carefully after first abandoning many of the preconceptions associated with such idea-words as *individualistic, moralistic, marketplace,* etc. In this case, for example, nineteenth-century individualistic conceptions of minimum intervention were oriented toward *laissez faire* with the role of government conceived to be that of a policeman with powers to act in certain limited fields. In the twentieth century, the notion of what constitutes minimum intervention has been drastically expanded to include such things as government regulation of utilities, unemployment compensation, and massive subventions to maintain a stable and growing economy—all this within the framework of the same political culture. The demands of manufacturers for high tariffs in 1865 and the demands of labor unions for workmen's compensation in 1965 may well be based on the same theoretical justification that they are aids to the maintenance of a working marketplace. Culture is not static. It must be viewed dynamically and defined so as to include cultural change in its very nature.

directly, favoring them even at the expense of others. In some political systems, this view is accepted by the public as well as the politicians.

Political life within an individualistic political culture is based on a system of mutual obligations rooted in personal relationships. While in a simple society those relationships can be direct ones, societies with I political cultures in the United States are usually too complex to maintain face to face ties. So the system of mutual obligations is harnessed through political parties which serve as "business corporations" dedicated to providing the organization necessary to maintain it. Party regularity is indispensable in the I political culture because it is the means for co-ordinating individual enterprise in the political arena and is the one way of preventing individualism in politics from running wild. In such a system, an individual can succeed politically, not by dealing with issues in some exceptional way or by accepting some concept of good government and then striving to implement it, but by maintaining his place in the system of mutual obligations. He can do this by operating according to the norms of his particular party, to the exclusion of other political considerations. Such a political culture encourages the maintenance of a party system that is competitive, but not overly so, in the pursuit of office. Its politicians are interested in office as a means of controlling the distribution of the favors or rewards of government rather than as a means of exercising governmental power for programmatic ends.

Since the I political culture eschews ideological concerns in its "business-like" conception of politics, both politicians and citizens look upon political activity as a specialized one, essentially the province of professionals, of minimum and passing concern to laymen, and no place for amateurs to play an active role. Furthermore, there is a strong tendency among the public to believe that politics is a dirty—if necessary—business, better left to those who are willing to soil themselves by engaging in it. In practice, then, where the individualistic political culture is dominant, there is likely to be an easy attitude toward the limits of the professionals' perquisites. Since a fair amount of corruption is expected in the normal course of things, there is relatively little popular excitement when any is found unless it is of an extraordinary character. It is as if the public is willing to pay a surcharge for services rendered and only rebels when it feels the surcharge has become too heavy.

Public officials, committed to "giving the public what it wants," are normally not willing to initiate new programs or open up new areas of government activity on their own recognizance. They will do so when they perceive an overwhelming public demand for them to act, but only then. In a sense, their willingness to expand the functions of government is based on an extension of the *quid pro quo* "favor" system which serves as the central core of their political relationships, with new services the reward they give the public for placing them in office.

The I political culture is ambivalent about the place of bureaucracy in the political order. In one sense, the bureaucratic method of operation flies in the face of the favor system that is central to the I political process. At the same time, the virtues of organizational efficiency appear substantial to those seeking to master the market. In the end, bureaucratic organization is introduced within the framework of the favor system; large segments of the bureaucracy may be insulated from it through the merit system but the entire organization is pulled into the political environment at crucial points through political appointment at the upper echelons and, very frequently, the bending of the merit system to meet political demands.

The Moralistic Political Culture

To the extent that American society is built on the principles of "commerce" in the broadest sense of the term and that the marketplace provides the model for public relationships in this country, all Americans share some of the attitudes that are of first importance in the I political culture. At the same time, substantial segments of the American people operate politically within the framework of two political cultures whose theoretical structures and operational consequences depart significantly from the I pattern at crucial points.

The *moralistic political culture* emphasizes the commonwealth conception as the basis for democratic government. Politics, to the M political culture, is considered one of the great activities of man in his search for the good society—a struggle for power, it is true, but also an effort to exercise power for the betterment of the commonwealth. Consequently, in the moralistic political culture, both the general public and the politicians conceive of politics as a public activity centered on some notion of the public good and properly devoted to the advancement of the public interest. Good government, then, is measured by the degree to which it promotes the public good and in terms of the honesty, selflessness, and commitment to the public welfare of those who govern.

In the moralistic political culture, individualism is tempered by a general commitment to utilizing communal—preferably nongovernmental, but governmental if necessary—power to intervene into the sphere of "private" activities when it is considered necessary to do so for the public good or the well-being of the community. Accordingly, issues have an important place in the M style of politics, functioning to set the tone for political concern. Government is considered a positive instrument with a responsibility to promote the general welfare, though definitions of what its positive role should be may vary considerably from era to era.[10]

[10] As in the case of the I political culture, the change from nineteenth- to twentieth-century conceptions of what government's positive role should be has been great, i.e., support for Prohibition has given way to support for wage and hour regulation. At the same time, care must be taken to distinguish between a predisposition toward communal activism and desire for federal government activity. For example, many M types oppose federal aid for urban renewal without in any way opposing community responsibility for urban redevelopment. The distinction they make (implicitly at least) is between what they consider legitimate community responsibility and what they believe to be central government encroachment, or between "communalism" which they value and "collectivism" which they abhor. Thus, on

The Moralistic Political Culture

Since the moralistic political culture rests on the fundamental conception that politics exists primarily as a means for coming to grips with the issues and public concerns of civil society, it also embraces the notion that politics is ideally a matter of concern for every citizen, not just those who are professionally committed to political careers. Indeed, it is the duty of every citizen to participate in the political affairs of his commonwealth.

Consequently, there is a general insistence that government service is public service, which places moral obligations upon those who participate in government that are more demanding than the moral obligations of the marketplace. There is an equally general rejection of the notion that the field of politics is a legitimate realm for private economic enrichment. Since the concept of serving the community is the core of the political relationship, politicians are expected to adhere to it even at the expense of individual loyalties and political friendships. Consequently, party regularity is not of prime importance. The political party is considered a useful political device but is not valued for its own sake. Regular party ties can be abandoned with relative impunity for third parties, special local parties, or nonpartisan systems if such changes are believed helpful in gaining larger political goals. Men can even shift from party to party without sanctions if the change is justified by political belief. In the M political culture, rejection of firm party ties is not to be viewed as a rejection of politics as such. On the contrary, because politics is considered potentially good and healthy within the context of that culture, it is possible to have highly political nonpartisan systems. Certainly nonpartisanship is not instituted to eliminate politics but to improve it by widening access to public office for those unwilling or unable to gain office through the regular party structure.[11]

---

some public issues we find certain M types taking highly conservative positions despite their positive attitudes toward public activity generally. M types may also prefer government intervention in the social realm—i.e., censorship or screening of books and movies—to similar government intervention in the economy.

[11] In this context, it should be noted that regular party systems are sometimes abandoned in local communities dominated by the I political

In practice, where the moralistic political culture is dominant today, there is considerably more amateur participation in politics. There is also much less of what Americans consider corruption in government and less tolerance of those actions which are considered corrupt, so politics does not have the taint it so often bears in the I environment.

By virtue of its fundamental outlook, the M political culture creates a greater commitment to active government intervention into the economic and social life of the community. At the same time, the strong commitment to communitarianism characteristic of that political culture tends to channel the interest in government intervention into highly localistic paths so that a willingness to encourage local government intervention to set public standards does not necessarily reflect a concomitant willingness to allow outside governments equal opportunity to intervene. Not infrequently, public officials will themselves seek to initiate new government activities in an effort to come to grips with problems as yet unperceived by a majority of the citizenry.

The M political culture's major difficulty in adjusting bureaucracy to the political order is tied to the potential conflict between communitarian principles and the necessity for large-scale organization to increase bureaucratic efficiency, a problem that could affect the attitudes of M culture states toward federal activity of certain kinds. Otherwise, the notion of a politically neutral administrative system creates no problem within the M value system and even offers many advantages. Where merit systems are instituted, they tend to be rigidly maintained.

The Traditionalistic Political Culture

The *traditionalistic political culture* is rooted in an ambivalent attitude toward the marketplace coupled with a paternalistic and

culture to institute nonpartisan electoral systems in an effort to make local governments more "business-like" and to take local administration "out of politics." Such antipolitical efforts are generally products of business-dominated reform movements and reflect the view that politics is necessarily "dirty" and illegitimate. In this context, see Edward C. Banfield, ed., *Urban Government* (New York: Free Press of Glencoe, 1961), Sections III and IV.

elitist conception of the commonwealth. It reflects an older, pre-commercial attitude that accepts a substantially hierarchical society as part of the ordered nature of things, authorizing and expecting those at the top of the social structure to take a special and dominant role in government. Like its moralistic counterpart, the traditionalistic political culture accepts government as an actor with a positive role in the community, but it tries to limit that role to securing the continued maintenance of the existing social order. To do so, it functions to confine real political power to a relatively small and self-perpetuating group drawn from an established elite who often inherit their "right" to govern through family ties or social position. Accordingly, social and family ties are paramount in a traditionalistic political culture, even more than personal ties are important in the individualistic where, after all is said and done, a person's first responsibility is to himself. At the same time, those who do not have a definite role to play in politics are not expected to be even minimally active as citizens. In many cases, they are not even expected to vote. Like the I political culture, those active in politics are expected to benefit personally from their activity though not necessarily through direct pecuniary gain.

Political parties are of minimal importance in T political cultures, since they encourage a degree of openness that goes against the fundamental grain of an elite-oriented political order. Their major utility is to recruit people to fill the formal offices of government not desired by the established powerholders. Political competition in a traditionalistic political culture is usually conducted through factional alignments, an extension of the personal politics characteristic of the system; hence political systems within the culture tend to have loose one-party systems if they have political parties at all.

Practically speaking, traditionalistic political culture is found only in a society that retains some of the organic characteristics of the preindustrial social order. "Good government" in that political culture involves the maintenance and encouragement of traditional patterns and, if necessary, their adjustment to changing conditions with the least possible upset. Where the traditionalistic political culture is dominant in the United States today, political leaders play conservative and custodial rather than initiatory roles unless pressed strongly from the outside.

Whereas the I and M political cultures may or may not encourage the development of bureaucratic systems of organization on the grounds of "rationality" and "efficiency" in government, depending on their particular situations, traditionalistic political cultures tend to be instinctively antibureaucratic because bureaucracy by its very nature interferes with the fine web of informal interpersonal relationships that lie at the root of the political system and which have been developed by following traditional patterns over the years. Where bureaucracy is introduced, it is generally confined to ministerial functions under the aegis of the established power-holders.

The "Geology" of Political Culture

The three political subcultures arose out of very real sociocultural differences found among the peoples who came to America over the years, differences that date back to the very beginnings of settlement in this country and even to the Old World. Because the various ethnic and religious groups that came to these shores tended to congregate in the same settlements and because, as they or their descendants moved westward, they continued to settle together, the political patterns they bore with them are today distributed geographically. Indeed, it is the geographic distribution of political cultures as modified by local conditions that has laid the foundations for American sectionalism. Sectional concentrations of distinctive cultural groups have helped create the social interests that tie contiguous states to each other even in the face of marked differences in the standard measures of similarity. The southern states have a common character that unites them despite the great material differences between, say, Virginia and Mississippi or Florida and Arkansas. Similarly, New England embraces both Maine and Massachusetts, Connecticut and Vermont in a distinctive way. These sectional concentrations can be traced for every part of the country, and their effects can be noted in the character of the economic interests shared by the states in each section.

The overall pattern of political cultures is not easily portrayed. Not only must the element of geography be considered, but also a kind of human or cultural "geology" that adds another dimension to the problem. In the course of time, different currents of migration have passed over the American landscape in response to the various frontiers of national development (see below). Those currents, in themselves relatively clear-cut, have left residues of population in various places to become the equivalent of geological strata. As these populations settled in the same location, sometimes side by side, sometimes overlapping, and frequently on top of one another, they created hardened cultural mixtures that must be sorted out for analytical purposes, city by city and county by county from the Atlantic to the Pacific.[12]

Quite clearly, the various sequences of migration in each locale have determined the particular layering of the cultural geology of each state. Even as the strata were being deposited over generations and centuries, externally generated events, such as depressions, wars, and internal cultural conflicts, caused upheavals that altered the relative positions of the various groups in the community. Beyond that, the passage of time and the impact of new events have eroded some cultural patterns, intensified others, and modified still others, to make each local situation even more

[12] A more detailed and elaborate discussion than can be given here of the origins and spread of the three subcultures will be found in the author's forthcoming book, *Cities of the Prairie*. Since the patterns of the political subcultures are tied closely to the patterns of the general subcultures in the United States, it is possible to gain some impression of the spread of the former from data prepared to illustrate the spread of the latter. One of the best sources for that data, though somewhat dated, is Charles O. Paullin's *Atlas of the Historical Geography of the United States* (Washington and New York: Carnegie Institution and American Geographical Society, 1932). The correlations between religious affiliation and political culture are clear and striking. Edwin S. Gausted's *Historical Atlas of Religion in America* (New York: Harper, 1962) includes maps showing the spread of religious denominations as of 1950, which are very useful in following the patterns of political culture as well.

complex. The simple mapping of such patterns has yet to be done for more than a handful of states and communities, and while the gross data which can be used to outline the grand patterns as a whole are available in various forms, they have been only partially correlated. However, utilizing the available data, it is possible to sketch with reasonable clarity the nationwide geography of political culture (Figure 3).

Political Culture and the Continuing Frontier

The geography of political culture is directly related to the continuing American frontier. Since the first settlement on these shores, American society has been a frontier society, geared to the progressive extension of man's control over the natural environment and the utilization of the social and economic benefits gained from widening that control, i.e., pushing the frontier line back. The very dynamism of American society is a product of this commitment to the conquest of the ever-advancing frontier, a commitment which is virtually self-generating since, like a chain reaction, the conquest of one frontier has led to the opening of another.[13] It is this frontier situation that has created the major social and economic changes which have, in turn, forced periodic adjustments in the nation's political institutions, changes of particular importance to the role and functioning of federalism and to the character and particular concerns of intergovernmental relations.

[13] The frontier process emerging from the meeting of civilization and raw nature is a dynamic one; men approach the untamed area with a view to bringing it under their control because it appears to offer indefinite possibilities for expansion as well as a chance to begin from the beginning, to implement goals which appear difficult or impossible to implement in the civilized area about them. A frontier situation possesses the following elements: (1) the exploration of that which was previously unexplored and the development of that which was previously undeveloped; (2) a psychological orientation toward exploration, development, growth, opportunity, and change—often typified in the "boom" spirit; (3) an economy that is growing in scope and changing in character; (4) manifold opportunities for exploration and pioneering, coupled with a strong element of risk; (5)

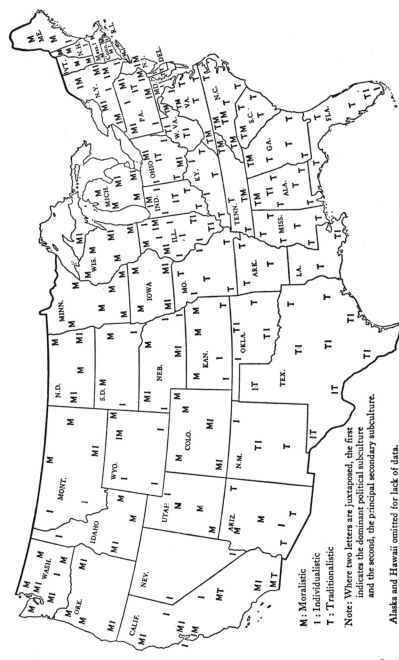

FIGURE 3. The Distribution of Political Cultures within the States

M : Moralistic
I : Individualistic
T : Traditionalistic

Note: Where two letters are juxtaposed, the first indicates the dominant political subculture and the second, the principal secondary subculture.

Alaska and Hawaii omitted for lack of data.

Since the opening of settlement in 1607, the American frontier has passed through three stages: First came the *rural-land* frontier—the classic American frontier described by the historians —lasting roughly from the seventeenth through the nineteenth centuries. It was characterized by the westward movement of a basically rural population interested in settling and exploiting the land and by the development of a socio-economic system based on agricultural and extractive pursuits in both its urban and rural components. Early in the nineteenth century, the rural-land frontier gave birth to the *urban-industrial* frontier, which began in the Northeast and spread westward, in the course of which it transformed the nation into an industrial society settled in cities and dedicated to the spread of new technology as the primary source of the nation's economic and social forms. The dominant characteristic of this frontier was the transformation of cities from service centers or workshops for the rural areas into independent centers of opportunity, producers of new wealth, and social innovators possessing internally generated reasons for existence and growth. At first overlapping the land frontier, the urban-industrial frontier became dominant by the last third of the century. By the midtwentieth century, it had given birth, in turn, to the *metropolitan-technological* frontier which is characterized by the radical reordering of an industrial society through rapidly changing technologies and a settlement pattern that encourages the diffusion of an urbanized population within large metropolitan regions. These radically new technologies, ranging from atomic

---

widespread freedom for people to engage in frontier-like activities and generally to have free access to the developing sector; (6) substantial movements of population in search of opportunity or improved living conditions; (7) an emergent or "unfinished" society that is continually responding to the advancing frontier by changing its social and settlement patterns; and (8) the creation of new opportunities on many levels of society as a consequence of pushing back the frontier. The basic statement of the frontier theory is still that of Frederick Jackson Turner and can best be found in his *The Frontier in American History* (New York: Holt, 1920). For an introduction to other aspects of frontier theory, see Nelson Klose, *A Concise Study Guide to the American Frontier* (Lincoln: University of Nebraska Press, 1964).

energy and automation to synthetics, and the accompanying suburbanization of the population influenced further changes in the nation's social and economic forms in accord with their new demands. Like the first two frontier stages, the metropolitan-technological frontier has also moved from east to west since the 1920's, becoming dominant nationally after World War II. Each successive frontier stage has opened new vistas and new avenues of opportunity for the American people. At the same time, each new frontier has brought changes in economic activities, new settlement patterns, different human requirements, political changes, and its own social problems that grow out of the collision of old patterns and new demands as much as they are generated by the new demands themselves.[14]

The basic patterns of political culture were set during the period of the rural-land frontier by three great currents of American migration that began on the east coast and moved westward after the colonial period. Each current moved, in the persons of the westward migrants, from east to west along more or less fixed paths, following lines of least resistance which generally led them due west from the immediately previous area of settlement.

Across the northern part of the United States thrusting westward and slightly southwestward is an area settled initially by the Puritans of New England and their Yankee descendants. The Puritans came to these shores intending to establish the best possible earthly version of the holy commonwealth. Their religious outlook was imbued with a high level of political concern,

[14] The history and significance of the American land frontier has been set forth in great detail by Turner and his students. See, for example, Turner, *op. cit.*, and Ray Allen Billington, *Westward Expansion: A History of the American Frontier* (New York: 1949). Much less has been written about the urban-industrial frontier. Two good studies are John Kouwenhoven, *Made in America*, rev. ed. (Garden City, N.Y.: Anchor Books, 1962) on the role of the new technology of the midnineteenth century and Anselm Strauss, *The Image of the American City* (Glencoe, Ill.: Free Press, 1961) on the urbanization aspects of the urban-industrial frontier. Walt W. Rostow's *The Stages of Economic Growth* (New York: Cambridge University Press, 1960) provides a theory of economic growth that strongly supports the hypothesis

in the spirit of the ancient Israelites whose ideal commonwealth they wished to reproduce. From the first, they established a moralistic political culture.

After five generations of pioneering in New England, where they established several versions of their commonwealth in the several New England states, the Puritans had developed a set of deeply rooted cultural patterns. Then, moving westward into New York State, the Yankees began their great cross-country migration. Across New York, northern Pennsylvania, and the upper third of Ohio, the Yankee current moved into the states of the upper Great Lakes and Mississippi Valley. There they established a greater New England in Michigan, Wisconsin, Minnesota, and Iowa, and they attempted to do the same in settling northern Illinois. Beginning in the midnineteenth century, they were joined by Scandinavians and other northern Europeans who, stemming from a related tradition (particularly in its religious orientation), reenforced the basic patterns of Yankee political culture, sealing them into the political systems of those states. Pressing westward, Yankees settled Oregon, then Washington, and were the first "Anglos" to settle California. As Mormons, they settled Utah; then as abolitionists they settled Kansas. They became the leaders of the permanent settlements in Colorado and Montana and even moved into northern Arizona. In all these states, they were joined or followed by the same Scandinavian–northern European group and in each they established the M political culture to the extent of their influence. Within those states and the smaller ones colonized from them, the moralistic political culture flourishes today.

Groups of quite different ethnic and religious backgrounds, primarily from England and the interior Germanic states, settled

presented here. The frontier aspects of the contemporary metropolitanization process have hardly been treated at all. The best discussion available is that of Samuel Lubell, *The Future of American Politics* (New York: Harper, 1952). See also, Daniel J. Elazar, *Some Social Problems in the Northeastern Illinois Metropolitan Region* (Urbana: University of Illinois, 1961). The author's forthcoming book, *Cities of the Prairie*, will contain an elaboration of the hypothesis presented here.

the middle parts of the nation, beginning with the Middle Atlantic states of New York, New Jersey, Pennsylvania, Delaware, and Maryland. The majority of these highly diverse groups, which together established the basic patterns of American pluralism, were united by one common bond in particular—the search for individual opportunity in the New World. Unlike the Puritans who sought communal as well as individualistic goals in their migrations, the pursuit of private ends predominated among the settlers of the middle states. Though efforts were made to establish morally purposeful communities, particularly in Pennsylvania, the very purpose of those communities was to develop pluralistic societies dedicated to individual freedom to pursue private goals, to the point of making religion a private matter, an unheard-of step at the time. The political culture of the middle states reflected this distinctive emphasis on private pursuits from the first and, by the end of the colonial period, a whole system of politics designed to accommodate itself to such a culture had been developed with distinctive state by state variations, modified by moralistic traits only in Pennsylvania and by traditionalistic ones in Maryland and Delaware.

These groups also moved westward across Pennsylvania into the central parts of Ohio, Indiana, and Illinois, then on into Missouri. There, reenforced by immigrants from western Europe and the lower Germanic states who shared the same attitudes, they developed extensions of their pluralistic patterns. Since those states were also settled by representatives of the other two political cultures, giving no single culture clear predominance, pluralism became the only viable alternative. So the individualistic political culture became dominant at the state level in the course of time while the other two retained pockets of influence in the northern and southern sections of each state.

After crossing the Mississippi, this middle current jumped across the continent to northern California with the gold rush (an activity highly attractive to I types). Its groups subsequently helped to populate the territory in between. The areas of Nebraska and South Dakota bordering the Missouri River attracted settlers from Illinois and Missouri; the Union Pacific populated central Nebraska and Wyoming; and Nevada was settled from the California gold fields. Today there is a band of states (or sections of states) across the belt of the country in which the individualistic political culture is dominant.

The people who settled the southern tier of states were seeking individual opportunity in ways similar to those of their brethren to the immediate north. But, while the latter sought their opportunities in commercial pursuits, either in business or in a commercially oriented agriculture, those who settled the South sought opportunity in a plantation-centered agricultural system based on slavery and essentially anticommercial in orientation. This system, as an extension of the landed gentry agrarianism of the Old World, provided a natural environment for the development of an American-style traditionalistic political culture in which the new landed gentry progressively assumed ever greater roles in the political process at the expense of the small landholders, while a major segment of the population, the slaves, were totally excluded from any political role whatsoever. Elitism within this culture reached its apogee in Virginia and South Carolina; in North Carolina and Georgia a measure of equalitarianism was introduced by the arrival of significant numbers of migrants from the M and I cultures, respectively.

This peculiarly southern agrarian system and its traditionalistic political culture were carried westward by the southern current. Virginia's people dominated in the settlement of Kentucky; North Carolina's influence was heavy in Tennessee; and settlers from all four states covered the southern parts of Ohio and Illinois as well as most of Indiana and Missouri. Georgians, with a mixture of other settlers, moved westward into Alabama and Mississippi. Louisiana presented a unique situation in that it contained a concentration of non-Anglo-Saxons rare in the South, but its French settlers shared the same political culture as the other southerners, regardless of their other cultural differences. Ultimately, the southern political culture was spread through Texas, where it was diluted on that state's western fringes by I type European in-migrants, and Oklahoma; into southern Kansas, where it clashed directly with the Yankee political culture; then across New Mexico to settle better than half of Arizona and overlap the Yankee current in southern and central California.

The only major departures from the east-west pattern of cultural diffusion during the settlement of the land frontier came when the emigrants encountered the country's great mountain systems. The mountains served to diffuse cultural patterns because they were barriers to easy east-west movement. Thus, in the east, the Applachian chain deflected the moralistic type Scotch-Irish southward from Pennsylvania where they were isolated in the southern mountains. There they developed traditionalistic patterns of culture over a moralistic base, and created special cultural pockets dominated by syntheses of the T and M cultures in the mountain areas of Virginia, the Carolinas, Georgia, and even Alabama.

In the west, the Rocky Mountains served to block the neat westward flow of the cultural currents and divert people from all three into their valleys from north to south in search of fortunes in mining and specialized agricultural pursuits. There the more individualistic types from all three subcultures diffused from Montana to Arizona, creating cultural pockets in all the mountain states of the west that in some cases—Wyoming, for example—altered the normal regional patterns of political culture.

The development of the urban-industrial frontier coincided with the arrival of other immigrant groups which concentrated in the burgeoning cities of the industrializing states. These groups, primarily from Ireland, Italy, eastern Europe, and the Balkans, also moved from east to west but settled in urban pockets adding new cultural strata to communities scattered throughout the country. Most of these settlers, though bound at first by traditional ties, soon adopted more individualistic attitudes and goals which brought them into the I political culture. Since most of them settled in cities, their cultural impact was less universal in scope but more concentrated in force. In some states (such as Massachusetts) they disrupted established cultural patterns to create new ones, in others (such as New York) they simply reenforced the existing I-dominant pluralism, and in still others (such as Illinois) they served to tip the balance between competing cultural groups.

The Contemporary Scene: Cultural Diffusion and the Metropolitan Frontier

Though the essential patterns of the three political cultures were set when the continent was first populated, the opening of the metropolitan technological frontier has kept them rather fluid in several ways. For one thing, migrations have continued. After the advent of the new frontier, Americans abandoned sedentary patterns widespread after 1910 and began to move again. Though their overall thrust is westward, these migrations from farm to city to suburb and from section to section no longer follow a simple east to west pattern. The first kind of migration usually takes place within the same section, if not the same states, leading to little alteration of the local patterns of political culture even as it may lead to substantial internal changes in the political culture itself. Iowans moving off their farms to Des Moines or Philadelphians moving from the central city to the suburban counties may simply reenforce existing patterns of culture. The second kind of migration may lead to the alteration of the cultural geology of particular areas—e.g., southerners moving to Detroit bring a traditionalistic political culture into a moralistic environment. In some cases, this movement cannot be identified as group migration, but in others the continuity of older modes of cultural diffusion and change is marked.[15]

California is a case in point. Its political culture remains in flux because of the continuous intensity of migration into the state, even though by the turn of the century, fairly well-defined cultural lines had been established within it. In a reversal of the

[15] One important study of the effects of these new migrations on American politics is Lubell, *op. cit.*, pp. 60–67, 75–78.

national pattern, southern California had become the center of the moralistic political culture because the Yankees and their midwestern descendants predominated there. Northern California, on the other hand, had attracted the Middle State migrants and had become the locus of the individualistic political culture, while central California was beginning to attract many southerners to give it strong traces of the traditionalistic political culture. The sharp cultural division between north and south (the central area was still too weak to be of importance) had already helped intensify the well-known conflict between the two sections of the state which came strongly to the fore in the Progressive era.[16]

Until recently, at least, the great migrations of the twentieth century have generally reenforced the original patterns of culture in California. Midwesterners from M culture states continued to seek the Los Angeles area, and I culture types, particularly from the east, the San Francisco Bay area. Each group has generally blended in well with the original political culture of its area of choice. Since Depression days, however, one substantial change has taken place. The increased migration of southerners into all parts of the state, with greatest intensity in the south and progressively less intensity moving northward, has added a strong strain of the traditionalistic political culture (or its particular individualistic manifestation which comes when its people leave their traditionalistic environment) in areas where that strain was weak or nonexistent. What has happened in those cases is the development of a conflict between the two political cultures as a consequence of the contrast between them.

While continued migration has helped keep culture patterns fluid, at the same time, the values of the various political cultures have undergone internal change. Moral demands have generally stiffened. For example, what is today considered "conflict of interest" in the M political culture was considered perfectly proper

[16] See George E. Mowry, *The California Progressives* (Berkeley: University of California Press, 1951).

in the days of Daniel Webster who, though an authentic Yankee, could take an annual retainer from a leading Boston bank while serving in the United States Senate, without any qualms. In another context, the I political culture, originally the home of the "rugged individualist," has taken on something of a collectivist tinge in the twentieth century as many of those within it have come to believe that "big government" offers opportunities for individuals unobtainable in any other way. Thus its representatives are often found at the forefront of the drive for greater government intervention into the economy. Meanwhile, the T political culture has tended to change into a form of individualism as its traditional social bases have been eroded. With its older elites no longer in positions of power because of economic and social changes, many of its traditionalistic attitudes have been transformed into bigotries designed to maintain the old racial caste system or unchallenged efforts to maintain the political status quo.

There is also a certain amount of assimilation from one culture to another based on changes in individual interests and attitudes. Under certain circumstances, cultural values change because of changing social status. There is some evidence that, as some people move upward into the middle- to upper-middle-class range, they may adopt at least some of the values of the moralistic political culture—which has always been a middle-class phenomenon—particularly if those values are the more acceptable ones in their communities. In true frontier fashion, this change often occurs in conjunction with a change of residence, such as migration to the suburbs. Thus it may be that as parts of New Jersey which were dominated by the individualistic political culture are being transformed into suburban areas, they are also being transformed into bases for the moralistic political culture. This is reflected in the rise of a new style Republican party which has gained a measure of power by opposing the old style "machine" politics of the Democrats and the GOP old guard, both of which symbolize the individualistic political culture in the least attractive form, on moralistic grounds.

The States and the Spread of the Political Cultures

The United States as a whole receives its distinctive character as a political system through an amalgam of the three political cultures. The individualistic biases of American society are strongly evident in the politics of every state and locality. At the same time, the highest offices in all three branches of the national government are defined by the public in moralistic terms, and the occupants of those offices generally accept that definition as the definitive one. Only the traditionalistic political culture appears to be declining as a force in American life, as the traditionalistic characteristics of southern society which supported it are being altered.

By now the reader has no doubt formed his own value judgments as to the relative worth of the three political subcultures. For this reason a particular warning against hasty judgments must be added here. Each of the three political subcultures contributes something important to the configuration of the American political system and each contains certain characteristics that are inherently dangerous to the survival of that system. The M political culture, for example, is the primary source of the continuing American quest for the good society. At the same time, there is a tendency toward fanaticism and narrow-mindedness noticeable among some of its representatives. The I political culture is the most tolerant of out-and-out political corruption, yet it has also provided the framework for the integration of diverse groups into the mainstream of American life. When representatives of the M political culture, in their striving for a better social order, try to limit individual freedom, they usually come up against representatives of the I political culture, to whom individual freedom is the cornerstone of their pluralistic order. Reversed, of course, the M political culture acts as a restraint against the tendencies of the I political culture to tolerate license in the name of liberty. The T political culture contributes

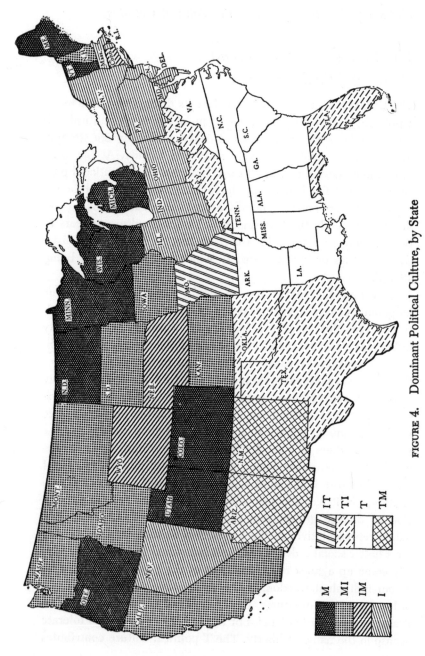

FIGURE 4. Dominant Political Culture, by State

to the search for continuity in a society whose major characteristic is change, yet in the name of continuity, its representatives try to deny Negroes their civil rights. When in proper working order, the T culture has produced a unique group of first-rate national leaders from among its elites, but without a first-rate elite to draw upon, T culture political systems degenerate into autocracies. Comparisons like these should induce a cautiousness in evaluation of a subject that, by its very nature, evokes evaluation.

It is equally important to use caution in identifying individuals and groups as belonging to one cultural type or another on the basis of their public political behavior at a given moment in time. While immediate political responses to the issues of the day may in themselves reveal the political culture of the respondents, they do not necessarily do so. Usually, deeper analysis of what is behind those responses is needed. In other words, the names of the political cultures are not substitutes for the terms "conservative" and "liberal" and should not be taken as such.

The amalgam of the political subcultures in the several states is varied, because just as all three political subcultures share in the nation's universal concerns, so representatives of each are found within every state. However, unique aggregations of cultural patterns are clearly discernible in each state. These cultural patterns give each state its particular character and help determine the tone of its fundamental relationship, as a state, to the nation. Figure 4 presents the particular pattern of political culture in each state while Table 11 presents the configuration of states on a nationwide scale. In general, the states of the greater South are dominated by the traditionalistic political culture; the states stretching across the middle sections of the United States in a southwesterly direction are dominated by the individualistic political culture; and the states of the far North, Northwest, and Pacific Coast are dominated by the moralistic political culture.

Seventeen states are predominantly or overwhelmingly influenced by the M political culture, sixteen are similarly influenced by the T political culture, and eleven by the I political culture. Of the others, three are borderline IM and one is borderline IT.

Table 11. State Political Cultures: The National Configuration [a]

SECTION	M	M-I	I-M	I	I-T	T-I	T	T-M
New England	Vt. Me.	N.H.	Conn.	Mass. R.I.				
Middle Atlantic				N.Y. Penna. N.J.	Del. Md.			
Near West	Mich. Wis.			Ohio [b] Ill. [b] Ind.				
Northwest	Minn. N.D. Colo.	Iowa Mont. Kan. S.D.	Neb. Wyo.					
Far West	Utah Ore.	Calif. Idaho Wash.		Nev.				
Southwest					Mo.			Ariz. N.M.
Upper South					Tex. Okla. W.Va. Ky. Fla.		Va. N.C. Tenn.	
Lower South						Ala. Ga. Ark. La.	S.C. Miss.	

KEY: M: Moralistic dominant.
M-I: Moralistic dominant, strong Individualistic strain.
I-M: Individualistic dominant, strong Moralistic strain.
I: Individualistic dominant.
I-T: Individualistic dominant, strong Traditionalistic strain.
T-I: Traditionalistic dominant, strong Individualistic strain.
T: Traditionalistic dominant.
T-M: Traditionalistic dominant, strong Moralistic strain.

[a] Alaska and Hawaii omitted for lack of data.
[b] Illinois and Ohio have strong traces of M in their northern counties and T in their southern counties.

NOTE: The eight columns in the table should be viewed as segments on a continuum that is actually circular. The specific placing of the individual states should be viewed cautiously, considering the limits of the data.

Table 12. Populations of the Cultural Groupings by State, 1940–1964 [a]

POLITICAL CULTURE [b]	NUMBER OF STATES	TOTAL POPULATIONS (IN MILLIONS)			
		1940	1950	1960	1964
M/MI	17	30,998	38,113	47,751	51,413
IM	3	3,276	3,624	4,276	4,589
I	11	53,000	59,060	68,457	72,053
IT	1	3,785	3,955	4,320	4,409
T/TM	16	39,947	45,167	52,915	57,102

[a] Alaska and Hawaii omitted for lack of data.

[b] For purposes of overall analysis, it is possible to combine the eight points on the continuum in Figure 7 into five categories.

These figures, which appear to give the M political culture the edge and place the I in a clear minority position, must be weighed against the relative populations of the states, shown in Table 12. The states dominated by the I political culture, though fewer in number, have by far the greatest share of the nation's population. While the aggregate population of the T states is growing in absolute numbers, their relative share of the nation's population is declining. Moreover, because several of them are undergoing subtle changes in the direction of the I political culture, the role of the traditionalistic subculture nationally is further diminished. In terms of population, the relative strength of the M states is increasing. The figures do not tell, however, whether the population increase in those states is reenforcing the established political subculture or injecting new elements foreign to it. Neither can the figures reveal to what extent the M political subculture is gaining strength in the I states as a result of social and cultural change.

Political Culture, the Frontier, and Sectionalism

The sectional pattern in the nationwide distribution of the political cultures is clearly visible in the maps and figures presented here. This is only one of the ways in which manifestations of sectionalism—the expression of social, economic, and political differences along geographic lines—are part and parcel of American political life. The more or less permanent arrangements that tie groups of contiguous states together as sections reflect the ways in which local conditions and differences in political culture modify the impact of the frontier. This overall sectional pattern reflects the interaction of the three basic factors. The original sections were produced by the variations in the impact of the rural-land frontier on different geographic segments of the country. They, in turn, have been modified by the pressures generated by that first and subsequent frontier stages. As a result, the sections are not homogeneous units sharing a common character that crosses state lines but complex entities that combine highly diverse states and communities which generally complement one another.[17]

Sectionalism is not the same as regionalism. The latter is essentially a transient phenomenon that brings adjacent states together because of immediate and specific common interests. The ten states ranging from Alabama to Pennsylvania that are crossed by the Appalachian Mountains and that have united to improve the lots of the depressed mountain communities on a regional basis provide a good example of regionalism. Their ties are expediential only, a product of their common interest in obtaining special federal assistance to overcome their respective problems of economic decline. Sectionalism involves arrangements of much greater permanence which persist despite the emergence of immediate conflicts or divergences among its components from time to time. For example, New England is a section bound by the tightest of economic and historical ties even though the differences between

[17] The classic work on sectionalism is that of Frederick Jackson Turner, particularly the collection of his essays published as *The Significance of Sections in American History* (New York: Holt, 1932). More recent works of importance include Merrill Jensen, ed., *Regionalism in America* (Madison: University of Wisconsin Press, 1951) and Harvey Perloff *et al.*, *Regions, Resources, and Economic Growth* (Baltimore: Johns Hopkins Press, 1960).

the states of lower New England (Massachusetts, Rhode Island,. Connecticut), which have been fully absorbed into the metropolitan-technological frontier, and those of upper New England (Maine, New Hampshire, Vermont), which are still in the process of being absorbed and retain much of their older character, are often more noticeable. There are, indeed, periodic conflicts between the two regions in New England. Nevertheless, the six states consciously seek to cooperate with one another in numerous ways, recognizing the bonds of both history and necessity. Thus Boston remains the economic and cultural hub of all but a fraction of southern New England. This alone makes it necessary for the six states to join together to deal with common problems of transportation, communications, education, and economic development.

Most sections have continuing intrasectional conflicts of long duration that persist within the context of their overall sectional unity in response to national concerns. For example, the intrasectional conflict between the states of the Far West over water resources, though a perennial issue, does not detract from their long-term community of interest in matters of commerce and education. More important for our purposes, certain common sectional bonds give the states of each section a special relationship to national politics, particularly in connection with those specific political issues which are of sectional importance; for example, the race issue in the South, the problems of the megalopolis in the Northeast, the farm problem in the Middle West, and the problem of federal land ownership in the Rocky Mountain states. One problem in understanding the influence of sectionalism on politics is the proper identification of those specific issues from among many apparent ones. During the heyday of the Populist movement, western and southern Populists made common cause against what they believed to be northeastern exploitation, despite the great cultural and even doctrinal differences between them. When the Populist movement failed, the temporary intersectional alliance came to an end for lack of binding common interests. Today certain students of American reform have failed to distinguish between the two kinds of populism simple because they were aligned at one point in time.[18]

Regionalism can often be a function of sectionalism. Indeed, each section can contain several regions just as some regions cross into several sections. For example, the interest of the northeastern states in gaining federal aid for urban rapid transit facilities is a temporary interest generated by an immediate problem. At the same time, it is a manifestation of the larger sectional tie fostered by the continuous urbanized belt from Maine to Virginia, often called the megalopolis, that has generated common problems in those states.[19]

Most attempts to discuss politics in regional or sectional terms are based on the regional scheme devised by the United States Bureau of the Census. While that scheme has its value, it is not necessarily the best, particularly for political analysis. For one thing, it ignores the regional patterns set by the three political subcultures. For another, it ignores the larger pattern of settlement in the country which is based on the linear thrusts of the frontier, usually westward.

The nation's sectional alignments are rooted in the three greater historical, cultural, and economic spheres into which the country is divided: the greater Northeast, the greater South, and the greater West. The three spheres can be outlined with nearly perfect accuracy by the three semi-circles indicated in Figure 5. Following state lines, the greater Northeast includes all those states north of the Ohio and Potomac Rivers and east of Lake Michigan; the greater South includes the states below that line but east of the Mississippi plus Missouri, Arkansas, Louisiana, Oklahoma, and Texas; and all the rest of the states compose the greater

[18] Richard Hofstader is one of the major students of American reform who succumbs to that kind of overgeneralization; see, for example, his *The Age of Reform* (New York: Knopf, 1955). See also Eric F. Goldman, *Rendezvous with Destiny* (New York: Knopf, 1952) for the history of the Populist alliance and its dissolution.

[19] Jean Gottmann, *Megalopolis: The Urbanized Eastern Seaboard of the United States* (New York: Twentieth Century Fund, 1961).

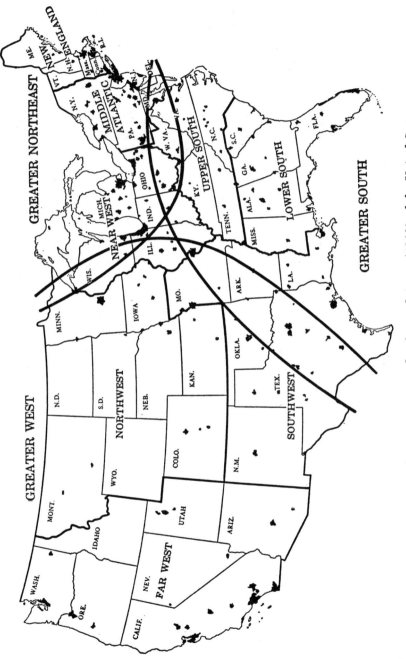

FIGURE 5.   Spheres, Sections, and Urbanized Areas (1960) of the United States (Hawaii, which has one urbanized area, is not shown.)

[115]

West.[20] Within that framework, there are eight sections constructed around two essential characteristics: (1) All reflect the linear thrust of the frontier generally opening to the west but, in a larger sense, opening from the heavily settled sectional heartland to its open hinterland. Thus, the Northwest opens from the Minneapolis–St. Paul area generally westward into Montana, New England opens from Boston generally northward, and the Far West—the one exception to the westward rule—from California generally eastward to the Rockies. (2) Each has sufficient internal diversity to reflect the social and economic complexity of the nation as a whole while also sharing sufficiently homogeneous cultural patterns to offer a unique variation of the national pattern.

Part of the response of each state to national politics and policies is related to the state's position in its section or sphere. Such responses are conditioned on whether a given state is a sectional leader, like Illinois, permanently subordinate, like South Dakota, or perpetually in opposition to the sectional leader, like Ohio; whether it possesses an "empire city," like Atlanta, that dominates the section, or is tributary to such a metropolis in another state; or whether the people have a greater stake in sectional or state concerns, generally or in regard to specific issues.

---

[20] Perloff, *op. cit.*, makes an excellent case for this scheme of spheres as the basis for the country's economic regions. See also Strauss, *op. cit.*, for a presentation of sociological evidence demonstrating the validity of this scheme.

It should be noted that between the points of intersection of the semicircles lie three areas—the Ohio Valley, the western South, and the western Great Lakes—which are transition zones between the spheres. Sharing the characteristics of two or more spheres, they have especially complex patterns of culture and politics.

CHAPTER FIVE

Varying Responses
to the Partnership

While there is no simple cause and effect relationship between the impact of political culture, sectionalism and the frontier, and the responses of the states to the intergovernmental partnership, the relationships between them are close enough to be worthy of further consideration. We have already touched briefly upon the influence of political culture on state governmental responses to federal grants-in-aid and to merit versus patronage systems. The influence of political culture on state responses to matters involving civil rights was touched on even earlier, albeit indirectly. Before turning to an examination of the influence of the combined factors, a few more important examples of the direct influence of political culture are in order.

The Clash of Political Cultures and Intrastate Unity

The juxtaposition of groups with different political cultures within the same political system, a product of the geology of cultural diffusion in the United States, has invariably led to some form of culture conflict within many of the states. In some, one political culture has been so dominant that representatives of other political cultures have never really been able to challenge its position. They have either assimilated into the dominant political culture or have established local pockets of the minority culture in the communities where they are in the majority. Thus representatives of the M political culture are clearly in the minority in Illinois, but, at the same time, they have been able to maintain an M political culture in Rockford, a city dominated by Yankees and Scandinavians.

In other states, two or more political cultures have been forced by circumstances to coexist within the same state, usually because each is strong among a substantial segment of population located in a particular section of the state. The struggle between the uplanders and lowlanders in the South Atlantic states, which has occasionally taken violent form and still remains a potent force in the politics of those states, has at least some of its roots in the clash of political cultures between the highlanders, who sought to participate as citizens in political affairs in the manner of the M political culture, and the gentry who represented the T political culture and saw every reason to retain its elitist patterns against all onslaughts. In Virginia, this struggle ultimately led to a formal division of the state. In North Carolina, on the other hand, the M types came into ascendancy, and though their political culture has been modified by southern values, they have given that state a unique position in the South. In South Carolina, the struggle goes on actively to this day, and the state's traditional division of its leading elective offices among candidates from the up-country and the coastal areas reflects the compromises it has induced for the sake of state unity.

In some of the older states on the eastern seaboard, established groups reflecting one political culture who have dominated state politics for generations have been inundated by in-migrants reflecting another. This is what happened in Massachusetts beginning with the mid-nineteenth century. The immigrant Irish, reflecting the individualistic political culture, assaulted the established Yankees and their moralistic political culture. The intensity of the Yankee-Irish conflict for political control since the late nineteenth century is a product of this clash between two very different political cultures which started from such radically different value premises. The sheer magnitude of the Irish immigration (and the other immigrations which shared the political attitudes of the Irish) has simply overwhelmed the Yankee commonwealth. Contrast this situation with the relatively harmoni-

Benedictine Library

Due Date 9/25/2014 09:00 PM

Title: American federalism; a view
         from the States [by] Daniel J.
         Elazar.
Author: Elazar, Daniel Judah.
Call Num 320.973 E37A
Enumera
Chronolo
Copy: 1
Item Bar

3 2 8 1 1 0 0 0 2 1 8 6 5 3

*Renew at www.ben.edu/library or (630)
829-6050*

ous amalgamation of Yankees and Scandinavians in Minnesota, where the ethnic conflict was confined within the same political culture and became a conflict for offices and status within a common value system.

Metropolitan-outstate conflicts obviously involve much more than the relatively simple issue of political culture, but in most states (Illinois and its relations with Chicago may be one exception) the cultural question is a mitigating or intensifying factor of some importance. In those states with major metropolitan centers that have attracted immigrant groups reflecting political cultures different from those dominant among the older population elements in the state as a whole, the metropolitan-outstate conflict has invariably been intensified beyond the relatively simple conflict between urban and rural economic interests. The reason is simple. Where men holding power believe that those seeking to displace them share their basic values, they are less likely to fear political change. However, when such change also promises to introduce men who will alter the very basis of the political value system—i.e., change the political consensus at its most crucial point—the intensity with which men will hold onto their positions is immeasurably increased. The conflicts between Boston and western Massachusetts or St. Louis and rural Missouri, where the cultural cleavage is great, are more intense than between Cincinnati and its Ohio hinterland or Minneapolis–St. Paul and outstate Minnesota, where there is no cultural cleavage of importance, at least partly because of the difference in their respective cultural situations. In cases where cultural conflict is important, the "outs" are likely to make use of any mechanisms available to gain power including—in a federal system—an appeal to the federal government to alter the political situation nationally so that they can gain their ends locally.

Political Culture and Voting Behavior

Since American elections, even national ones, are based substantially on local concerns and are conducted by state and local party organizations, to the extent that political culture and conflicts between political cultures influence political behavior in the states, they become important in determining state responses to national politics.

Citizen participation in politics as measured by voting turnout clearly reflects the different predispositions in the fifty states based on their particular political cultures. It is reasonably clear that people who believe they can accomplish something positive through the political process are more likely to vote and otherwise become active in politics than those having little faith in the efficacy of politics.[1] Thus it would be natural for M types to be most active, T types to be least, and I types to fall somewhere in between, responding to specific elections differently.

In presidential elections, states of the M political culture consistently lead in percentage of voters turning out, reflecting the internalization of those cultural norms by the citizenry at large. Moreover, most of the states of the I political culture that approached the M states in turnout have strong M minorities—particularly those New England states once dominated by M types in which a cultural synthesis may now be developing. The I states, on the other hand, show no clear-cut overall pattern as a group, a situation which is as it should be since the difference between high and low turnout in those states depends on the activity of political organizations or particular idiosyncratic situations that attract voters to the polls. Finally, the T states have the lowest level of turnout (even without considering the Negro voting problem) as befits a culture which holds that political participation is not demanded of the many but is kept in the hands of the few. There is considerable evidence that as certain southern states lose their traditionalistic political culture as a consequence of post-World War II developments, voting turnout increases.[2]

[1] Lester W. Milbrath discusses this problem and summarizes the available research on the subject in *Political Participation* (Chicago: Rand McNally, 1965).

[2] Complete data on turnout are available for the period since 1920 in the Report of the President's Commission on Registration and Voting Participation (November 1963).

Where comparative data are available, the evidence shows that the same general distribution holds true for state elections as well as presidential ones.[3]

The M and I states generally make voting registration easier than the T states, though for slightly different reasons. The M states wish to encourage broad political participation for all those who will put forth a minimum amount of effort to become participants, while in the I states, there is a convergence between this view and the interest of the political organizations to make voting as easy as possible for the segment of the population they influence most.

Election campaign costs also appear to be influenced by variations in political culture. Logically such costs should be larger in the larger states with the most urbanized populations or in states with the highest levels of voter participation. In fact, such evidence as we have indicates that, on a per capita basis, campaign costs are higher in the states dominated by the traditionalistic political culture where money can be used as an incentive to bring voters to the polls because there are few other direct incentives and the culturally supported norms do not encourage voting for participation's sake. Thus Kentucky and Tennessee spend more per capita and even in absolute figures in statewide elections than California, no doubt reflecting the widespread local custom of paying for votes in the former two states.[4] The system of vote-buying in West Virginia has received national publicity. This custom is also widespread in the traditionalistic sections of the I-dominated states located north of the Ohio River.

Kinds of political participation also seem to reflect cultural predispositions though here the evidence is less clear. While M types tend to turn out heavily to vote and may even decide to run for office or serve in some other civic capacity, they are less likely to take an active role in political organizations or campaigning. They appear to take a more literal view of the citizen's political

[3] See Milbrath, *op. cit.*
[4] Alexander Heard, *The Costs of Democracy* (Chapel Hill: University of North Carolina Press, 1960), p. 425, Table 56.

Table 13. Political Culture of the States and Interparty Competition

ONE-PARTY DEMOCRATIC	MODIFIED ONE-PARTY DEMOCRATIC	TWO-PARTY	MODIFIED ONE-PARTY REPUBLICAN
South Carolina (T)	Virginia (Ti)	Alaska	Wisconsin (Mi)
Georgia (T)	North Carolina (Tm)	Missouri (IT)	New Hampshire (Mi)
Louisiana (T)	Tennessee (Tm)	Rhode Island (Im)	Iowa (Mi)
Mississippi (T)	Oklahoma (IT)	Washington (Mi)	Kansas (MI)
Texas (TI)	Kentucky (TI)	Delaware (It)	Maine (Mi)
Alabama (T)	Arizona (TM)	Nevada (I)	South Dakota (MI)
Arkansas (T)	West Virginia (TI)	Massachusetts (Im)	North Dakota (Mi)
Florida (TI)	Maryland (It)	Hawaii	Vermont (M)
	New Mexico (TI)	Colorado (Mi)	
		Montana (Mi)	
		Minnesota (M)	
		Utah (M)	
		Connecticut (IM)	
		Pennsylvania (Im)	
		California (MI)	
		Nebraska (IM)	
		Illinois (Itm)	
		Idaho (MI)	
		Michigan (Mi)	
		New Jersey (Im)	
		Indiana (It)	
		Oregon (Mi)	
		Ohio (Imt)	
		Wyoming (IM)	
		New York (Im)	

NOTE: The classification of the states in regard to interparty competition is adapted from Austin Ranney's adaptation of the Dawson-Robinson Measure as used in Herbert Jacob and Kenneth N. Vines (eds.), *Politics in the American States* (Boston: Little, Brown, 1965), Chapter 3. Symbols in parentheses indicate a state's political culture (lower-case letters indicate minority culture). The states are listed in descending order, with South Carolina the most solidly Democratic, Hawaii the most competitive, and Vermont the most solidly Republican.

role as one of participating in the formal channels of political activity rather than in the less formal ones. I types, on the other hand, if interested in politics at all, can be recruited for the kinds of campaign work generally considered by contemporary students of politics to be the basic form of political participation. T types participate either in every facet of government or in none, depending upon whether they are members of the right elites.

Political culture appears to influence the level of interparty competition in the states (see Table 13). It has already been mentioned that the states most influenced by the T political culture are most likely to be one-party states. This is true even in those states in which the problem of excluding Negroes is not of central importance. Since single-party dominance is less in those T states influenced by other political cultures, it is not unreasonable to conclude that there is a connection between political culture and the character of the states' party systems. This connection is less apparent in the M and I states. Since both types represent post-traditional societies, the differences in the character of their party systems are based on more subtle phenomena. Still, the states with modified one-party Republican systems are all dominated by the M political culture, reflecting certain complex ethnic and historic factors which encouraged votes from that political culture to identify with the GOP for many years.[5]

The States in Congress

It has already been noted (Chapter One) that the states dominated by the T political culture (mainly in the South) tend to be most unified internally on issues of nationwide concern and most differentiated from the nation as a whole. The unique cultural characteristics of the South have been widely discussed, and many

[5] For a discussion of party competition in the states, see Austin Ranney, "Parties in State Politics," in Herbert Jacob and Kenneth N. Vines, eds., *Politics in the American States* (Boston: Little, Brown, 1965), Chapter 3.

writers have characterized those differences as stemming from the South's traditionalistic attitudes in a nation that has moved far from the patterns of a traditionalistic society.[6] The one-party system that has flourished in the southern states for more than a century, sustained by local political culture as well as national political need, has contributed to the well-known and well-documented ability of the South to gain more than its proportionate share of benefits from Washington while surrendering least to the pressures that emanate from the nation's capitol.[7] This is only partly because one-partyism has given the South a leg up through the congressional seniority system. Indeed, the southerners' habit of retaining their congressional representatives flies in the face of the intense factionalism found in many of the southern states. It is, instead, a measure of their understanding of the workings of the American partnership, an understanding born of their traditionalistic approach to the art of politics. They know that seniority is useful because it brings benefits to their states. It brings benefits because southern congressmen use their time to develop their personal positions in the web of government to the point where they are able to pull strings whenever and wherever necessary to get what they want, in the manner of traditionalistic politics. So states otherwise faction ridden display great internal unity when it comes to maintaining their senators and representatives in Washington.[8]

Most of the states highly unified internally but also strongly in agreement with national policies and programs are those either

[6] The southern subculture has been the most thoroughly studied of the three cultures. The best of these studies is found in W. J. Cash, *The Mind of the South* (New York: Knopf, 1940). For a comparison and contrast between the original northern and southern subcultures, see William R. Taylor, *Cavalier and Yankee* (New York: Braziller, 1961).

[7] In 1963, for example, according to *Congressional Quarterly* calculations, Florida was the only southern state to receive relatively less in federal grants than its share of the federal tax burden.

[8] It is only necessary to note how men with equal seniority who came from states dominated by other political cultures behaved when in similar situations. Contrast, for example, the activities of the senior Republican senators from the North with the senior Democratic senator from the South

dominated by the M political culture or strongly influenced by it. Their minority political culture unites them against any "outside encroachment" that might seek to inject elements of a different kind of *politics*. Yet at the same time, they do not necessarily have fundamental *policy* differences with the federal government (at least on the domestic front). In the late nineteenth and early twentieth centuries, before the New Deal, there was often a great deal of conflict between the policies their representatives advocated and those adopted by the federal government. These states were in the forefront of the third-party movements that appeared and reappeared at all levels of government in the two generations following the Civil War, and a roster of the nation's Progressive leaders is heavily weighted with the names of their representatives.[9]

Though most of these states are among the smaller ones and the younger ones in the Union, they have, on the whole, contributed more than their proportionate share of the men in Congress with national rather than regional or local reputations. The national figures from these states have usually been active in promoting social welfare and reform programs or have, in exceptional cases, acquired reputations as "consciences of the nation." A major share of their abilities is frequently directed toward the achievement of national goals or the enactment of legislation of nationwide impact, while activities designed to gain special con-

---

sixty years ago when one-party systems were more prevalent in the former region, seniority was about equal, and the Republicans were in power most of the time. Even when the Republicans did use their seniority to gain special benefits, they were more often than not benefits for their immediate supporters, not for their states or the people of their states.

[9] See Eric F. Goldman, *Rendezvous with Destiny* (New York: Knopf, 1952). The New England Puritan influence was of great significance in shaping virtually every one of the Progressive leaders, even, in many cases, those from states dominated by I political cultures. See Stewart Holbrook, *The Yankee Exodus* (New York: Macmillan, 1950). Under the right circumstances, the old Populist-Progressive bloc periodically reappears. Thus, the outspoken senatorial opponents of American involvement in Viet Nam have, with few exceptions, come from the tier of states stretching from Wisconsin to Oregon that produced the "sons of the wild jackass" of two and three generations ago.

sideration for their states, their party organizations, or their personal associates are distinctly secondary. To the extent that this kind of behavior has been widespread among congressional delegations in certain states, those states have lagged behind the others in benefiting from federal spending. At the same time, these M representatives have been stirred by particular kinds of local problems that have, for them, a quasi-moral focus, and for these state needs they have worked diligently and successfully on Capitol Hill. Thus, with some significant exceptions they have generally poor records in securing defense installations. Their record in the water resource development and natural resource conservation fields is entirely different, as their states, east and west, have benefited from river development projects and conservation programs of all sorts.[10]

The states least unified internally are those that have strong competing cultural currents within their limits. In general, they are also least differentiated from national patterns in policy matters and tend to be dominated by the I political culture. The I-dominated states are invariably two-party states whose senators, elected statewide, rarely accumulate great seniority but whose representatives may if they have more homogeneous districts.[11] The apparent "liberalism" of the dominant political forces in

[10] The exceptions prove the rule. The three states of this group whose representatives have actively endeavored to secure the expenditure of federal defense funds within their limits—California, Colorado, and Washington—have been eminently successful. These three states, like the others in this group, have been equally, if not more, successful in the water resource and conservation realm. The best simple source verifying this is the official map of the United States and its public lands published by the Bureau of Land Management, Department of the Interior, Washington, D.C.

[11] The reasons for this are more complex than indicated here. The character of the states' party organizations often means that men must wait until middle age before aspiring to a senate seat, after working their way up through the ranks or establishing themselves as "names" in other spheres of activity and then being brought in to head a "blue ribbon" ticket. The position of these states as national centers often means that candidates for national office, elective and appointive, are chosen from the ranks of their congressional delegations. Review of the data on seniority in Donald R. Matthews, U.S. Senators and Their World (Chapel Hill: University of North Carolina Press, 1960) with these variables in mind will indicate how this is so.

these states today is often a reflection of perceived economic self-interest rather than a commitment to any abstract principles of social welfare or reform. When it comes to securing benefits, their representatives in Congress tend to exert themselves for individuals—constituents, political associates, individual business or community interests—rather than for their states. At the same time, their representatives are in a position to attract a great deal of public attention in the nation as a whole because of the size and influence of the states (and big cities) they represent.

Sectionalism and the States' Position in the Union

Every one of the examples cited in this chapter and Chapter Four has a sectional component. Indeed sectionalism has been an accepted fact in American life for many years. Though its importance has been somewhat obscured since the days of the New Deal, when public attention turned to the problems of an industrialized society, many of the sectional differences of the past have begun to reemerge in new guises, to affect American politics on a broad front.[12]

Sectionalism both unites the states in matters of sectional concern and makes it more difficult for them to maintain themselves as political systems. While the existence of the federal system forces most sectional problems into the framework of state boundaries, most of the features that distinguish one section from another do not follow state lines. Figure 6 indicates this elemental

[12] The popular but erroneous notion that sectionalism has all but disappeared as a political force is based, in part, on the myth that sections in the nineteenth-century heyday of sectionalism were separated by different public concerns. In truth, they shared the same universal concerns then and their differences, then as now, stemmed from differing attitudes toward those concerns and differing notions of how to deal with them. The various regional studies of state politics, cited elsewhere in this volume, are quite useful in understanding the present-day political impact of sectionalism. Theodore H. White applies an interesting regional scheme as part of his analysis of the 1960 presidential election in *The Making of the President, 1960* (New York: Atheneum, 1961), which is useful as an introduction to the political impact of American sectionalism.

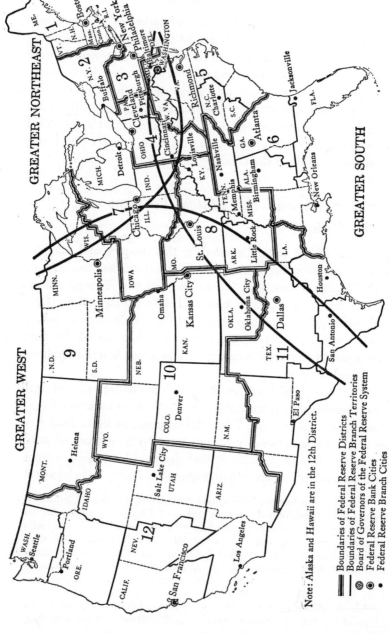

FIGURE 6. Boundaries of Federal Reserve Districts and Their Branch Territories

Note: Alaska and Hawaii are in the 12th District.

Boundaries of Federal Reserve Districts
Boundaries of Federal Reserve Branch Territories
Board of Governors of the Federal Reserve System
Federal Reserve Bank Cities
Federal Reserve Branch Cities

fact clearly. The scheme of federal reserve districts, one of the most accurate regional schemes in use today, reveals empire cities and their cohorts searching for, settling, and drawing from the largest possible hinterlands without regard for state lines. To a certain extent, then, this aspect of sectionalism operates to weaken the states. The actively directed search for hinterlands, pushed by every chamber of commerce, like the less directed spread of political cultures or the natural endowments of soil and water that determine where the corn belt or the wheat belt is best located, is no respecter of state boundaries. The history of the drawing of the federal reserve district boundaries in 1912 and 1913 is a case in point. The nation's leading cities competed for designation as reserve bank cities (i.e., district headquarters) and those that won them had districts drawn to reflect their spheres of influence, regardless of state lines.

A perennial problem of the states, hardly less important than that of direct federal-state relationships, is how to bend sectional and regional demands to fit their own needs for self-maintenance as political systems. When those demands are reenforced by the interests of the nation's great cities, that task is made even more difficult. Since the concern with regional development is now growing, this difficulty is being magnified. One of the ways in which the states are able to overcome this problem is through the use of the formal political institutions they control. In the first place, the formal institutions are the major features distinguishing one section from another that do follow state lines. The states themselves are formal institutions performing that role. So are their respective systems of local government (see Chapter Seven). The states are protected to the extent that no regional problems can be handled governmentally without making use of those formal institutions. Thus the representatives of the states use the formal institutional structure to influence federal action to handle problems in such a way as to allow the states a role.

The latest federal plans for formal regionwide action are being drawn with just such considerations in mind. The new Appalachia program will be managed by a state-federal commission consisting of representatives of the Appalachian states and the federal government sitting as equals which will supervise the redevelopment of that region. At this writing, similar programs are being developed for other depressed regions in other sections of the country. Contrast this approach with that of the federal government in developing the Tennessee Valley Authority during the centralizing days of the early New Deal. The TVA was established as a unilateral federal project charged with cooperating with the states but not formally subject to their influence. In point of fact, the TVA has cooperated very closely with the states in which it operates, strengthening their capabilities as political systems at many points. Still, Congress has never authorized another such unilateral program, and federal regional development programs since the 1930's (all of more limited scope) have made increasingly greater provisions for state representation at the policy-making level. Whether the Appalachia approach will prove to be a method that meets state as well as regional needs remains to be seen.

Some would argue that the use of formal political institutions to deflect sectional patterns on behalf of the states is "artificial" interference with the "natural" flow of the nation's social and economic system. Partisans of the states would respond not only by questioning the naturalness of a socio-economic system that was created by people who migrated freely across the landscape as individuals in search of opportunity but by arguing that the history of civilization is the record of man's efforts to harness his environment by means of his inventions, all artificial in the literal and real sense of the term. It need not be pointed out that political institutions are among the foremost of those inventions.

Sectionalism and the Metropolitan Frontier

Sectional differences have considerable influence in determining when and how a concern that is ultimately nationwide in scope actually arises in particular states. The spread of the urban and metropolitan frontiers and the concerns endemic to each are illustrative. Public discussion of urban problems in the United States generally assumes a sameness in the character of those problems from coast to coast. In one sense, when urbanization and metropolitanization each began in earnest, cities or metropolitan areas sprang up in every settled part of the country. In the beginning, however, their respective impacts were clearly greater in the northeastern states. Ultimately, each spread westward to the Great Lakes states, jumped to the West Coast, and then moved into the trans-Mississippi Middle West and southward. As the respective frontiers engulfed each section at different times, each section and each state within it developed somewhat different patterns of urban life (and politics), depending upon the character of its economic organization, technology, public taste, migrational patterns, and the like.[13]

Today, metropolitanization is a particularly acute and universal problem in the northeastern states where it has led to the formation of a megalopolis crossing state lines and complicating the situation for the states as political systems. In the Great Lakes and Pacific Coast states, though metropolitanization has become dominant, the projected megalopolitan complexes of the East Coast type have yet to emerge. Metropolitan complexes in those states do not embrace whole sections and are rarely interstate. More localized, they vary according to the size of the metropolis and, in any case, are limited to the sections' metropolitan communities. Metropolitanization in the South has taken a different form, one more characteristic of that section and more in keeping with the political systems of its states. There, a pattern of scattered medium-size metropolitan settlements punctured by a few big centers is the rule, and while every southern state has much the same kind of metropolitan problems, their problems are quite different from those of the great metropolitan

---

[13] For a history of American urbanization, see Charles N. Glaab, *The American City: A Documentary History* (Homewood, Illinois: Dorsey Press, 1963). For a discussion of some of the differing effects of urbanization in the several sections, see Anselm Strauss, *op. cit.*

states elsewhere. Actually, most southerners still live outside the metropolitan areas, considerably lessening the impact of the problem. The scattering of metropolitan areas in the greater West, from Chicago to the Pacific, has led to the development of a heirarchy of cities of all sizes generally fitting into a regionwide pattern produced originally by the organization of the entire sphere's economy around rapidly spreading railroads and since reenforced by new means of transportation.[14] This means that the states of that region are affected differently by metropolitanization because their cities have grown in connection with continental patterns rather than local ones. Some states, like Colorado and Washington, have several metropolitan areas, including ones of a million or more people, which began their development a century ago in response to the locational demands of western settlement. Others, like the Dakotas, have just one small metropolitan area which has only recently emerged as a result of the general growth in population and economic complexity. In the greater West, the problems of metropolitanization are not only less intense than "back east" but are not even similar in the various states within the region.[15]

Similarly, there are substantial sectional differences today in both the context and format of urban growth. In the Northeast and Near West, central cities are declining in population while the suburbs are growing. In the Northwest, both central cities and suburbs are growing. In the South, new metropolitan areas are emerging and, in a number of cases, are consolidating metropolitan governmental functions at the county level in the traditional southern pattern of reliance on county government. In the Southwest, major annexation programs are extending central cities at the expense of suburban areas, transforming the former into very large municipalities.

[14] See *Rand McNally Commercial Atlas* (Chicago: Rand McNally, published annually) for a projection of the nation's metropolitan pattern by size and an excellent ranking of American cities by economic importance.

[15] For data on the varying patterns of growth, annexation, and consolidation, see the *Municipal Yearbook*, published annually by the International City Managers Association, 1313 E. 60th St., Chicago, Illinois.

Table 14. *Percentage of Population Living in Urban Places in Twenty
Selected States, 1960*

STATE	PERCENT-AGE	U.S. RANK	STATE	PERCENT-AGE	U.S. RANK
New Jersey	88.6	1	California	86.4	2
Rhode Island	86.2	3	Texas	75.0	7
New York	85.4	4	Utah	74.9	8
Massachusetts	83.6	5	Arizona	74.5	9
Connecticut	78.3	6	Nevada	70.4	14
Maryland	72.7	12	Washington	68.1	15
Pennsylvania	71.6	13	New Mexico	65.6	18
Delaware	65.7	17	Oklahoma	62.9	21
New Hampshire	58.3	26	Colorado	62.7	22
Maine	51.3	34	Minnesota⎱Oregon⎰	62.2	24

SOURCE: U.S. Bureau of the Census.

Because of all this diversity, the need for political action to
meet most metropolitan problems must necessarily vary from section to section, both in kind and in scope. State responses to those
needs vary accordingly, ranging from the active state participation in urban transportation and redevelopment programs characteristic of New York and Pennsylvania, through the willingness of
state authorities to allow their big cities to take action on their
own as in Illinois and Ohio, to state-level resistance to similar
urban efforts as in Georgia and Nebraska. While these responses
are not uniformly sectional, the sectional influence is very strong
because of the sectional distribution of metropolitan patterns.

Many of the variations in state political behavior usually
ascribed to urbanization must be explained in terms of sectional
and cultural differences in the impact of the urban frontier. A
look at the percentage of population living in urban places in
twenty selected eastern and western states (Table 14) in conjunction with a map of population concentrations will illustrate
this point clearly. The states of the Rocky Mountain West are
highly urbanized, yet their political behavior bears little resem-

blance to that of the urbanized northeastern states. Urbanization in the western states reflects the existence of an "oasis culture" whereby the bulk of the desert, semidesert, or just plain open land of that section remains generally unpopulated while the people congregate in the few hospitable oases where living can be made tolerable by cooperative effort.[16] It does not necessarily reflect an urban culture in the sense of a desire for the kind of classic urban living in the European image or as described by urban planners. It simply reflects the westerners' need to congregate in cities even when engaging in not-very-urban pursuits such as mining and agribusiness.

The western attitude can be characterized as the national attitude writ large. Americans take to metropolitanization easily as an extension of the center-hinterland relationship characteristic of American sectionalism, even as they tend to reject city-style living. Indeed, many American cities were metropolitan—in the sense of being centers for large regions—long before they became urban. Today this attitude is apparent in state after state. The people have moved to cities of varying sizes located within metropolitan areas but the pattern throughout the country is to suburbanize (or even "ruralize") those cities as much as possible to prevent them from becoming "citified." [17] This means, among other things, that state and national political alignments which favor cities are not necessarily desired, even by city residents in those sections. Reference to Table 4 (pp. 28–31) indicates that the alignment on legislative apportionment is not simply urban-rural but the industrial big cities against the rest of the country.

This factor is potentially a powerful instrument in the hands of the states in their periodic contests with the big cities. If the urban interests are not as closely connected to urbanism as believed and if those interests which are really urban are not as widely shared as believed, then the impact of urbanism on the

[16] The "oasis culture" of the prairie plains West has been described in some detail by Walter Prescott Webb in *The Great Plains* (Boston: Ginn, 1931). A look at a map of the United States showing the variations in population density will confirm this pattern, which has intensified in the past several decades.

[17] For a fuller discussion of this, see Strauss, *op. cit.*

position of the states will be different than many today anticipate. As yet, however, few of the states have shown any inclination to consciously shape their activities to appeal to this "agrarian" interest within metropolitan America or to develop programs that will help maintain something of the desired agrarian way of life in face of the very real social problems of urbanization that confront the nation.

A Summarizing Case

The record of state legislation in the civil rights field prior to recent federal action sums up much of the interaction between the aforementioned factors and the political struggle in the states. At the end of 1961, no antidiscrimination legislation existed in the southern states, no matter how urbanized. Two of the border states, semiurban Kentucky and West Virginia, had established official state human relations commissions and a third, highly urban Missouri, had acted to outlaw discrimination in employment. In the North and West, all but three states had legislated in some form against discrimination, but the extent of their actions seemed to be dependent on something other than either the percentage of Negroes in their respective populations or the extent of urbanization. Table 15 lists the fifteen states with the most comprehensive antidiscrimination legislation. Eight of the ten northern and western states with the largest Negro populations had full or substantial coverage, among them four predominantly of the M political culture and three of the others with substantial M minorities. But seven states with few Negroes had coverage equally comprehensive, five of which were dominated by the M culture and the other two, originally dominated by that political culture, with influential M minorities. Seven of the ten most urbanized states are in this group but the remaining eight range from eleventh to twenty-fifth in urbanization.

In every one of the foregoing fifteen states it was a combination of the moralistic political culture plus the existence of a high degree of ethnic diversity that led to this kind of legislation. The affected ethnics, in effect, challenge the majority to live up to the

Table 15. State Antidiscrimination Legislation through 1961 and Other Variables

STATE	PERCENTAGE NEGRO	U.S. RANK	PERCENTAGE URBAN	U.S. RANK
1. States having full coverage [a]				
Massachusetts	2.2	32	83.6	4
Connecticut	4.2	27	78.3	6
New York	8.4	18	85.4	3
Pennsylvania	7.5	20	71.6	14
Minnesota	0.7	41	62.2	25
Colorado	2.3	31	62.7	23
Oregon	1.0	38	62.2	25
2. States having substantial coverage [b]				
Rhode Island	2.1	33	86.4	2
New Jersey	8.5	17	88.6	1
Michigan	9.2	15	73.4	11
Indiana	5.8	23	62.4	24
Illinois	10.3	14	80.7	5
Wisconsin	1.9	35	63.8	20
Washington	1.7	37	68.1	16
California	5.6	24	86.4	2

[a] Includes antidiscrimination legislation in the fields of public accommodations; employment; public and public-assisted housing; private housing; and education.

[b] Includes four or five of the above provisions.

SOURCES: U.S. Bureau of the Census (1960) and U.S. Civil Rights Commission, Report (1962).

demands of their political culture and virtually embarrass them into doing so. In this respect, the northern New England states which do not have that kind of diversity have not been challenged to "fulfill" this demand even within the context of their M political culture.

The Frontier and Federalism

In the years since 1961, the complexion of governmental activity in the civil rights field has undergone great changes nationally and in the states. These changes represent the culmination of pressures for Negro equality generated by the metropolitan-technological frontier. Until the post-World War II period, agitation for equal and unsegregated treatment for Negroes was confined to a small minority in both the Negro and white communities. The war itself created new sources of support for the elimination of racial discrimination by broadening the horizons of many Americans, including many Negroes, and by forcing the American people to restate the nation's traditional goals of liberty, equality, and justice as part of their confrontation with fascism. But it was in the postwar world that the decisive factors leading to the Negro revolution were formed. It would be difficult to identify, much less list, all those factors, but there is general agreement that (1) Negro demands were strengthened by the South's efforts to attract new industry and the resultant urbanization of that section. Stated in terms of the hypothesis advanced here, the well-nigh inevitable advance of the urban-industrial frontier southward upset the established patterns of a rural society to stimulate the demands of those victimized by that society. (2) Negro demands were reinforced by the impact of television, a product of the metropolitan-technological frontier, which brought an awareness of the larger world into nearly every Negro home, and gave them a sense of the possibilities of participation in that world. In general, the new material prosperity of the nation generated by the metropolitan frontier made the demands for equality all the more urgent in both the North and the South. Furthermore, the frontier-generated social and political revolution that ended white Anglo-Saxon Protestant domination of American society held out new hope to the groups still kept in second-class citizenship because of race.[18]

Government responses were also accelerated by the metropolitan-technological frontier. The new demands for educated manpower were highly influential in overthrowing old legal

[18] For a study of the rise of the new pluralism after World War II, see Will Herberg, *Protestant–Catholic–Jew* (Garden City, N.Y.: Anchor Books, 1955).

doctrines of racial segregation in the schools on the grounds that equal educational opportunities had become the primary path to social and economic equality in a society facing accelerated technological change. The opening of a new frontier of settlement for whites in the suburbs raised questions of the necessity for government action to create equal opportunities in housing for non-whites that were kept buried in the days when substandard housing was the lot of most urban dwellers. And so the list goes.

The many governments of the United States have had to respond to these frontier-generated demands by changing old patterns and recasting certain traditions. The governmental response was in keeping with the long-established tradition of similar responses to other frontier situations. All levels of government were under pressure to act where they could, and, by and large, all have taken steps in the direction of insuring equal rights through legal action. In the South, however, massive resistance to such steps caused the federal government to take on a coercive role. This, in turn, has made it seem as if the new frontier were leading to an expansion of federal power at the expense of the states. With this superficial view in mind, it is easy to conclude that the frontier process is acting as a centralizing force in the civil rights field.

In this respect, the civil rights issue can be viewed as a paradigm of other frontier-generated movements toward increased governmental activity. There is no question that the frontier process places new challenges in front of the states, just as it does for every level of government. At least in this country, the frontier and federalism have had a unique interrelationship. The federal-state relationship is a product of the frontier situation in early American history and, at the same time, is molded anew by the frontier process in successive generations. The frontier generates change which, in turn, demands new governmental responses; hence, the specific roles of the several governments also change over time. Viewed without historical perspective, the changing roles frequently appear to represent the encroachment of one level upon the prerogatives of another, when, in reality, they may simply reflect a temporary dislocation of established re-lationships on the way to the reestablishment of a new federal balance. Whenever all levels of government are able to respond in concert to the new demands, the balance is restored as before (though invariably with a higher level of governmental activity across the board). Only when objective conditions limit the abil-ity of one level or another to respond is there a shift in the real locus of power within the federal system.

In the case of civil rights enforcement, the ultimate sharing of power is still not certain. Even as the federal government has been stepping up its activities, so have the states, particularly in the North and the West. Those states that had been ahead of the national government in 1961 have generally maintained their lead by strengthening their civil rights laws and enforcement proce-dures. Other states, under the twin stimuli of internal pressures from local civil rights groups and the potential intervention of federal authorities under recent national legislation, are enacting legislation of their own which will enable them to retain control over civil rights enforcement within their boundaries but on a new level. In this way, these particular demands of the new fron-tier are being met, still within the framework of federalism.

Along with the civil rights issue, the metropolitan frontier has also created new tensions in the federal system in regard to the proper role of the three levels of government in education. Education, considered an important governmental responsibility for well over a century, has always received some support from every level of government. Today, however, its importance has taken on a new meaning as a result of the new frontier's demands for higher levels of skills and the greater costs of education in a more complex society. Here, too, old intergovernmental arrange-ments have been challenged by the objective demands of new situations. Local school districts are consolidated to establish larger schools able to offer more comprehensive programs. Seek-ing more financial aid, they turn to the state for funds, and the states, in turn, uses their power of the purse to set higher standards for the local districts to maintain. Simultaneously, both the states and their local subdivisions are turning to Washington for even more money while the professional educators wish to use federal aid to improve education qualitatively as well as to support it quantitatively. The states are also taking action to coordinate their policies on an interstate basis to obviate the necessity for federal intervention in policy matters. Here, too, the future shape of governmental sharing is as yet undetermined, depending in part on objective conditions beyond the control of any government.

CHAPTER SIX

Protecting the States' Integrity

The constitutional compact binding the federal government and the states clearly provides for federal supremacy and gives the federal authorities the power to maintain that supremacy. Moreover, in a complex world, the very pervasiveness of the sharing system gives the powerful federal government means to dominate the states in many ways, if it chooses to do so. At the same time, the traditions which have grown up around the constitution, while not negating this federal power, have tempered its use by inducing a policy of federal self-restraint and providing the states with political means for the maintenance of that policy.

The States, the Supreme Court, and the Electoral System

The states are best able to protect themselves and to induce federal self-restraint when the problems confronting them are handled through regular political channels and are least able to do so when the problems are not, constitutional guarantees notwithstanding. Thus the federal institution that has done most to limit the states' powers is the United States Supreme Court, which, because of the American commitment to an independent judiciary, benefits extraordinarily from its position as the final judicial arbiter of the Constitution. For example, the United States Supreme Court has recently taken it upon itself to act as the ultimate arbiter of the very basis of legislative representation—the drawing of electoral districts for choosing state and national legislators —by extending the Fourteenth Amendment dictum of "equal protection of the laws" to reflect the currently popular notion that political democracy must rest directly in every case on the doctrine that each person's vote must be weighted equally on a population basis. The Court has seen fit to do this despite clear constitutional provisions granting Congress the power to regulate congressional elections and a history of congressional legislation in the field, plus nearly as clear a reservation to the states of the final power to determine the character of the apportionment of their own legislatures plus its own precedents of self-restraint.[1] The consequences of the Court's entrance into the political thicket of legislative apportionment are not yet clear. What is clear is that in this case as in so many others, accepted prerogatives of the states are being challenged by the one institution that is least subject to control through the normal channels of politics and that the Court's right to do so is not being seriously challenged even by those who oppose the decision.[2]

Even with the entrance of the Court into the apportionment question and the increasing concern of all three branches of the federal government with protecting the rights of Negroes to vote in the southern states, voting in all elections—federal, state, and local—remains essentially a state-regulated activity providing the states with a *de facto* bulwark against overextension of federal

[1] The most important decisions were *Baker* v. *Carr*, 369 U.S. 186 (1962); *Gray v. Sanders*, 372 U.S. 368 (1963); *Wesberry v. Sanders*, 376 U.S. 1 (1964); and *Reynolds* v. *Simms*, 377 U.S. 533 (1964) with its companion cases. The written opinions of the justices involved in the case examine the issue from many sides. Justice Harlan's dissent in the *Reynolds* case is particularly useful as a review of previous constitutional doctrine on the reapportionment question.

[2] To say the courts are least influenced by politics is not to say that they are uninfluenced. On the contrary, the standard pattern of recruiting judges from among active politicians has helped make the courts more sensitive to the nuances of the political process than might otherwise be the case. Indeed, at the lower court levels, the sensitivity of judges often works in the states' favor to neutralize less sensitive high court decisions. See Jack W. Peltason, *Federal Courts in the Political Process* (New York: Random House, 1955) and John R. Schmidhauser, *The Supreme Court: Its Politics, Personalities, and Procedures* (New York: Holt, Rinehart & Winston, 1960).

authority, a bulwark subject only to the explicit restrictions placed on it by the Fifteenth, Nineteenth, and Twenty-fourth Amendments of the United States Constitution, the relatively few acts of Congress regulating voting, and the Court decisions interpreting same. Until the passage of the Voting Rights Act of 1965, it was quite clear that Congress actually exercised more control over federal elections a century ago than it does today. Even that act reflects considerably more federal self-restraint than the voting legislation passed during Reconstruction, and, if the states that are potentially affected by the act continue their trend toward compliance, the actual amount of federal enforcement in the field will be minimal. In any case, within the context of the Constitution, all the states retain the right to determine the number, times, and places of elections within their boundaries, and the overwhelming majority of the states also retain full control over age and residence requirements.[3]

The States, the Parties, and Congress

Clear state responsibility for the organization and regulation of the party system has strengthened the role of party politics as a guarantor of state integrity. Given formal status through state law in the first instance, the party system has been legitimized only tangentially through judicial interpretation or even federal legislation. The Supreme Court has seen fit to confine its role in the legal regulation of political parties to providing general standards of guidance for the states, such as prohibiting the "white primary," a device for preventing Negro voters from effectively exercising their right of franchise and insuring the right of parties to have the votes for their candidates counted fairly. Thus the political parties, which may be considered state associations that are made national through the development of interstate coalitions, have been given national constitutional status without any altera-

[3] See V. O. Key, Jr., *Politics, Parties, and Pressure Groups*, 5th ed. (New York: Crowell, 1964), Chapter XXII.

tion of their initial structure except that imposed by the states themselves.[4]

The representation of the states in Congress provides another very important way for them to maintain their integrity and internal autonomy, through a highly institutionalized system of congressional interference into executive actions. To understand this system, it is necessary to look briefly at the growth of administrative rule-making powers.

The discretionary rule-making power of federal administrative agencies has been substantially increased to the point where their rule-making activities have nearly as much effect on state-federal relations as formal legislation and judicial interpretation. The sheer mass of federal business has made this necessary. Congress can, at best, set forth the general guidelines for implementing federal-state programs, awarding contracts, or administering federal programs that touch upon the individual directly. Once these guidelines are established, however, federal administrators must make the specific rules and then apply them. The individual states, in turn, have found that they must have some means of recourse to influence the way in which those rules will affect them, short of trying to alter the general legislation.

The representatives of the states have found such a recourse in the institutionalization of "interference" (the term is used in a neutral sense) into the national administration. The formalization of procedures for legislative oversight of the administration is relatively recent, and is presently embodied in the Legislative Reorganization Act of 1946. Yet the tradition of such interference is well developed, dating back to the very beginning of the Republic. There are two kinds of interference. Best known is the formal system of legislative oversight with its tradition of insuring a place on key committees for representatives of states and even localities most seriously affected by the actions of those committees and their counterparts in bureaucracy. This has given the states an important line of access to national policy-making, through the powers of the committees to review proposed legislation and in-

⁴ *Ibid.*

vestigate ongoing programs and through the powers of committee members to demand consideration for their constituents and constituencies as the price for supporting the adminstration. Considering the important role of the committees, this institution has indeed become a crucial one in the perpetuation of the noncentralized traditions of American federalism.[5]

The states and localities not only possess virtual representation on committees; their interests are also represented by their congressmen acting singly. Very early in the history of the Republic, congressmen and their constituents interpreted the right of petition as the right to interfere in administrative affairs on behalf of their constituents—private or public—establishing the right of congressional interference as part of the nation's unwritten constitution. With the increased bureaucratization of the federal executive branch, this interference, or "casework" as it has come to be called, has only the barest connection with the original constitutional right. It is basically a political device rooted in the power of local groups over their elected representatives and the desire of the latter to build up credit with potential supporters. Considering only its effects on the relations between the states and localities and the federal government, it is a most useful device for gaining administrative consideration for state and local needs *after* legislation has been enacted and at the point where administrative discretion in statutory interpretation comes into play.[6] Congressional staffs, which have grown in size primarily because of this responsibility, handle their casework with great care, knowing that their congressman's performance in that area is often likely to influence more voters than his actions on remote national issues. Administrative agencies also go to great lengths to serve congressional interests and, by indirection, the interests of

[5] See J. Leiper Freeman, *The Political Process: Executive-Legislative Relations* (New York: Random House, 1955) for further discussion of the role of the committee system.

[6] Kenneth E. Gray has made a thorough study of casework which is summarized in "Congressional Interference in Administration," a paper presented at the 1962 annual meeting of the American Political Science Association in Washington, D.C. This section draws heavily on his work.

[145]

the individuals, groups, states, and localities the congressmen represent, because they know that future congressional support is often dependent on this kind of service rather than on an assessment of the effectiveness of an overall program whose very complexity discourages understanding.

While the great majority of the cases which lead to congressional interference do not involve other governments, they are nonetheless important to the maintenance of the position of the states and their local subdivisions. Just because the states are civil societies, the actions and requests of ostensibly private parties are often highly meaningful for the maintenance of state and local authority or for the development of a state's public policy. Thus a request by a chamber of commerce for the expansion of a local military installation or a private manufacturer's bid for more government contracts may well reflect calculated effort on the part of the state and local leaders—if not governments—to promote the development of their "little" economies. If this form of subnational governmental influence is an as yet barely recognized aspect of American federalism, it is no less a real one and an important adjunct to the maintenance of the position of the states.

The extent to which any state takes advantage of the opportunities available to it through congressional interference does not appear to follow any recognizable pattern. In one sense, every congressman is so involved in casework that the differences among the states are marginal. In another sense, some states organize more actively than others to handle state problems in Washington. The congressional delegations of several states meet together regularly (often once a week) to plan ways and means to serve the interests of their states. While this kind of cooperation is easier in one-party states and is most prevalent among the southern delegations whose members are past masters at interference, states with very competitive two-party systems, such as California, Massachusetts, and Colorado, also unite in Washington, without regard for party lines, in matters of statewide interest. For many states, internal political fights stop at the state line and are replaced by a "bipartisan foreign policy" vis-à-vis Washington.[7]

Administrative Rule-making and Program Implementation

Perhaps paradoxically, administrative rule-making often has a decentralizing effect that extends the powers of the states in shared programs even beyond those actually authorized by congressional legislation and interference. Good relationships that develop between federal and state (or local) administrators often allow the state people to gain even more freedom of maneuver than is given them formally by law.

The politics surrounding the administration of the cooperative grant-in-aid programs demonstrate this forcefully. It has been said that "Grants-in-aid are programs for which the states have responsibility but in which the entire nation has an inter-

[7] Here the states with greater internal unity, as shown in Table 2, have the advantage, all other things being equal. Indeed, this ability to cooperate in dealing with Washington was one of the measures considered in compiling that table. But even apparently disunited states can maintain a "bipartisan foreign policy" if they make the effort. Massachusetts is a case in point. Two decades ago, the state's leaders on both sides of the political fence discovered that, by carrying their partisan concerns over to Washington, they were failing to get things done for the state as a whole. Despite their intense partisan differences within Massachusetts, they agreed to unite when outside of its boundaries "for the good of the Commonwealth" and have been functioning as a bipartisan unit on the Washington scene ever since, with the success indicated earlier in Chapter Three. Even more unusual was the agreement between Colorado's two senators, one from each party, during the 1930's and 1940's whereby they shared a joint office for Colorado affairs and handled all casework problems jointly. This and other examples of state lobbying in Washington are discussed in Morton Grodzins, "American Political Parties in the American System," *Western Political Quarterly*, XIII (December 1960), 974–98. States actually do have long-term "foreign policy" interests, some of which have persisted for over a century. This writer has identified such concerns for over thirty of the states.

est." [8] Through the conditional transfer of funds to the states, the federal government gains a voice in making policy in those fields aided by the grants while the states remain responsible for day-to-day administration of the programs with all that the responsibility implies in the way of actual policy-making. Though the conditions attached by Congress and the federal administrative agencies in the name of Congress are unquestionably important ones, federal control is practically lessened by the powers of state government utilized by state agencies to preserve areas of discretion within which they remain free to act relatively unencumbered by outside rules and regulations.

Each state is responsible for planning its own programs, preparing the requisite budgets, enacting the necessary legislation, promulgating the regulations, and appropriating the funds needed for carrying them out. At this level, federal influence is applied through several sets of formal mechanisms. The legal terminology of the federal law and the administrative rules and regulations applying the law offer the most direct bases for federal influence. The amount of money made available to the states by Congress in most cases controls the scope of each year's program. With these tools in hand, the federal agency charged with administering the grants for each program has to review all relevant state laws, rules and regulations, plans, performance manuals, and budgets, to certify that they conform to the requirements of federal law as the agency interprets it. If the state is adjudged to have failed to meet federal requirements, the federal authorities may take several steps to enforce compliance: by rejecting the findings of audits and reviews, by withholding payments due the state, or, in extreme cases, by withdrawing all federal funds.

Because the federal authorities are hesitant about using harsh methods that might end or seriously weaken programs they are anxious to see maintained, these formal mechanisms are put

[8] The quotation is from E. Lester Levine, "Federal Grants-in-Aid: Administration and Politics," unpublished research outline, April 1964, p. 1. This discussion draws heavily upon Mr. Levine's research and analysis.

into play through the informal devices of consultation and persuasion, applied even before the formal ones are used. Federal officials seek cooperative compliance on the part of the states through such methods knowing that such compliance is more effective in the long run. To develop this atmosphere of cooperation, they are prepared to make concessions to their state counterparts.

While the foregoing paragraphs discuss federal regulations and state compliance in terms of potential conflict, the general atmosphere that pervades the programs is one of cooperation. Uppermost in the attitudes of most federal and state officials involved in the cooperative programs is the sense of partnership in a common endeavor. This means that a federal official from a regional office charged with insuring state compliance with federal regulations does not visit his state counterpart as an inspector but as a "cooperator" (the term is commonly used in the federal agencies). Moreover, the frequency and character of such visits vary from periodic casual meetings that fulfill the letter of the law in programs where the state people are trusted, to regular, careful inspections where standards have not yet been fixed or their maintenance is in doubt. Often the primary purpose of such visits is to enable the federal people to offer technical assistance in areas of their competence though that depends upon whether the state officials need or welcome such outside aid. In any case, the federal agencies can and do serve to disseminate information of mutual interest among the states.

The decisions of the professional administrators in the federal service who are charged with overseeing specific programs are shaped by many factors, including the personalities of the men involved and the character of their commitment to the program they are administering. In the end, what usually happens is that the federal and state officials, working in the same programs, trained in the same schools, and active in the same professional associations, think along the same lines more often than not and have relatively little trouble in reaching a meeting of minds on technical questions.

The state agencies are undoubtedly influenced by the afore-mentioned formal and informal mechanisms when formulating and implementing their programs, but they, in turn, can modify that influence through several channels. First of all, they can use the system of congressional interference of which they are a part. Congressmen find state agencies important to them in their efforts to serve constituents because those agencies are uniquely able to combine professional expertise and sensitivity to local needs. Levine states the matter succinctly: "[T]here are federal agencies who give him [the congressman] facts and local constituents who tell him what they want. The state agency understands local wants and yet also has the facts the Congressman needs." [9]

Thus the state agencies can be of help to their state's representatives in Washington and, in the process, gain influence simply by being what they should be—men in the middle with access to both sides. In return, the congressmen will often help a state agency by securing additional funds for the grant program it handles, by working for changes in federal legislation which the agency wants in order to simplify its tasks or enhance its position, or, in unusual cases, by assisting the agency in its efforts to change federal administrative decisions where the state body is embroiled in conflict with its federal counterpart. Of the three forms of congressional assistance, the first is the most common and, in one sense, the one that gives the states the most leverage vis-à-vis the federal bureaucracy. In many cases, a federal agency administering a certain grant program is dependent upon the state agencies it is supposed to supervise to secure the funds it is to disburse (or even the funds it needs to operate). The possibilities of leverage inherent in this should be obvious.

A second channel open to the state agencies is through their national professional associations. There are many such associations. Indeed, it would be difficult to find a field of governmental service whose professionals do not have one. The quality and strength of these associations varies considerably. The strongest are also the best organized. These often include organizations of

[9] *Ibid.*, p. 3.

ex officio state officials such as the American Association of State Highway Officials or the Association of State and Territorial Health Officers. However, associations ostensibly composed of professionals in their private capacities, such as the American Library Association and the American Public Welfare Association, often represent state agency interests. Federal officials are frequently active members of these associations where they meet with their state counterparts on truly equal terms to influence and be influenced—as well as to simply enjoy each other's company. In fact, many of the associations are even encouraged by the federal government.

These professional associations do much to influence federal and state agencies alike by setting standards and conducting research. Consequently many of the ostensibly "Federal" rules applied to the states are really "federal" in origin—shaped by the associations of professionals serving the states and localities as well as the federal government, whose responsibility it is to implement the very same programs. The standards governing the construction of federal-aid highways are devised by the American Association of State Highway Officials working in cooperation with the Bureau of Public Roads. Similarly, the National Education Association and the American Association of State Universities have major roles in shaping the rules for implementing the various federal educational aid programs. The same situation prevails in most of the major cooperative programs. If they wish to secure changes in federal regulations or standards, state agencies, then, can work within their professional associations where they stand on equal terms with the federal members.

The importance of this power to set standards cannot be minimized. In a complex society, neither federal nor state legislators have sufficient expertise to do more than set broad policy guidelines in most fields. For the detailed standards that set the tone of day to day operations, they must rely upon experts. Thus the administrator as expert holds crucial power in the program.

The professional associations act as arms of the states by mobilizing expertise and political "muscle" in other ways. By utilizing their combined expertise to provide technical assistance to state agencies, they enable the states to gain expert knowledge without depending upon federal technicians. In another role, the state agencies often lobby in Washington for legislative changes and larger appropriations for "their" programs or for entirely new programs through their professional associations. The present federal grant program for improving library facilities, beginning with the 1955 Rural Library Services Act, is largely the product of the efforts of the American Library Association pressed by the state library associations, just as the interstate highway program was planned and promoted by the American Association of State Highway Officials.

A third channel used by the states to maintain their integrity in managing shared programs is, very simply, well-organized state government. States with sound and up-to-date administrative structures, strong cadres of professionals in the various fields of state concern, centralized budgetary and administrative practices, and a strong chief executive have many ways to gain mastery over the grant (and other) programs if they desire to do so. It must be reiterated, though, that the cooperative nature of the system and the sense of partnership pervading it means that federal officials are not loath to allow such states much greater leeway. When the professional qualifications of the state and local personnel involved in a given program are established, their federal counterparts are apt to regard their views as equally valid and respectable and to give them great leeway in managing even the federal funds granted for their programs. If the federal administrators are also sympathetic to the idea of noncentralized government, as many, if not most, of them are, they are even more likely to minimize their use of the powers they are entitled to exercise.

When federal and state administrators are in general agreement as to the "right" way to implement particular programs, the states are most likely to be given a free hand. But even when federal administrators "go by the book," their state counterparts are frequently able to avoid further investigation by submitting the requisite formal documents applying for funds and accounting for their use in the approved manner. If the documents meet the requirements, no further investigations are conducted and the state agencies then go their own way in actually using the funds, having "bought" freedom from real supervision. As a general rule, the better established a program is, the less likely it is that federal administrators will exercise the supervisory powers legally theirs.[10]

In a sense, the least effective way for the states to influence the direction of established cooperative programs is through the formal institutions normally considered the bulwarks of state autonomy, particularly the state legislatures. Practically speaking, the legislatures exercise the same legal or formal controls over most federally aided programs as they do over those financed exclusively by the state. They must appropriate the states' share of the funds, enact the necessary legislation, create the requisite agencies, and authorize the employment of the personnel needed to staff them.[11] Utilizing all these powers, the legislatures can exercise considerable control if they choose to do so. In fact, however, the legislators are faced with a perennial psychological conflict. They want to get as much federal money as possible even as they wish to resist any involvement with the federal government which most of them are not in a position to influence. In the end, they may pick and choose between smaller programs and they may even refuse to appropriate enough state money to match all the federal funds available, but they rarely exercise any decisive influence on the cooperative arrangements. Their role re-

[10] Governmental Affairs Institute, *A Survey Report on the Impact of Federal Grants-in-Aid on the Structure and Functions of State and Local Governments,* submitted to the Commission on Intergovernmental Relations (Washington: Government Printing Office, 1956).

[11] Employment security funds which are obtained through a federally administered tax on employers are not appropriated by the legislature, under the law, but are formally controlled by the governors. The same is true of certain other contracted federal funds.

mains significant only indirectly, as overseers of the state administrative structure and as a source of authority for the operating agencies, but it is not the role that it could be.[12]

Guarantees of State "Republicanism"

While the political process has been put to hard use to find ways to guarantee state political integrity against the pressures of centralization, virtually nothing has been added to the constitutional guarantees that allow federal authority to be used to maintain representative government within the states. It has been determined that Congress has the exclusive authority to decide whether a state has "a republican form of government" by accepting or refusing to seat the state's elected representatives. It has also been clear that Congress will rarely exercise its powers in this respect. Though not couched in these terms, the recent Supreme Court decisions in the realm of reapportionment may possibly be viewed as an effect to establish criteria of "republicanism" and to enforce them through federal intervention.

The greatest opportunity for federal action to cloak these guarantees with meaning came a century ago during the Civil War, yet only minimal reliance was placed upon them at that time, either to restore the Union or to reconstruct the seceding states. The various cases of federal military intervention within the states have rarely, if ever, been justified under any of those guarantees. In the one or two cases when states have apparently abandoned representative government in spirit, they have retained the forms of republicanism and no effort has been made to invoke federal power or even to exclude the states' representatives from Congress.

In reality, then, such guarantees as exist stem from outside

[12] The weakness of the legislatures in this regard and the parallel weakness of state governors who simply do not have the time or staff assistance to closely supervise the operations of the grant programs allow the state agencies to gain a measure of autonomy from their own central governments, often playing the federal government against their state supervisors for their own advantage.

the written Constitution, having their source in the nationwide party system and the process by which it has induced the penetration of national concerns into the states. While these may appear to be imperfect, short-range guarantees, in the long run they have proven quite effective in breaking or at least lessening the grip of autocracies and oligarchies which from time to time have assumed power in various states to frustrate the spirit of republicanism, simply by preventing the states from developing a politics fully divorced from the national scene. The universality of political concerns in the United States and the use of the party system to develop nationwide responses to those concerns has meant that the internal political systems of every state have at least had to assimilate certain nationally approved devices for meeting those concerns. The mechanisms of the secret ballot, for example, have been adopted by every state from ethnically heterogeneous Pennsylvania to oligarchical Virginia to racist Mississippi to middle-class oriented Colorado. In the process, a common level of "republicanism" as presently defined in the country as a whole has been introduced in each of those states.[13]

The one major addition to the written Constitution which has had profound effects on the position of the states in the federal union is the package of Civil War amendments, the Thirteenth, Fourteenth, and Fifteenth. That package formally ratified the supremacy of the national government along the lines set forth

---

[13] Mississippi in 1965, a state as far removed from national standards of republicanism as any state has ever been, is an excellent and highly visible example of how this works. Observers have described it as virtually a police state. Yet, with all the quasi-totalitarian and violent means of repression being used within that state to maintain the "Mississippi way of life," outside pressures are enabling Negroes to register and vote, a write-in campaign for Negro candidates for public office was mounted in 1963, and a Negro-sponsored "Freedom Democratic Party" from Mississippi won substantial recognition at the 1964 Democratic National Convention. Because of the nationwide character of presidential politics and nationwide concern over civil rights, the severely repressed Mississippi Negroes are able to mobilize politically as Mississippians, within their state and in the national arena, and with outside support are slowly able to improve their position within Mississippi.

in federalist political theory as embraced by the Yankee North.[14] By transferring power to the North, it made possible the ultimate ascendancy of the moralistic and individualistic political cultures at the national level, to replace the traditionalistic political culture which had been so influential on the national scene in the pre-Civil War years. It also provided the constitutional basis for the expanded federal supervision of state actions in the field of civil and political rights in recent decades.

Even these three wartime amendments, passed in a period of national crisis with the express purpose of asserting federal supremacy by providing Congress with the power to enforce that supremacy, were ultimately fitted into the system of noncentralization through the political process. As Reconstruction ended, the restoration of southern representation in Congress and the emergence of the "Solid South" made it possible for the ex-Confederates to virtually eliminate congressional or executive action to enforce many of the provisions of those amendments. Faced with the potentialities for federal action inherent in the war amendments, the southerners were forced to devise ways to keep these potentialities from being translated into action. Control over the choice of presidential candidates by the Democratic party through the two-thirds rule, the development of the seniority system in Congress, and the use of the filibuster in the Senate gave the southern states much of what John C. Calhoun had advocated a generation earlier—the right to demand concurrent majority decisions in all matters affecting their vital sectional in-

[14] The problem of competing theories of Federalism and their sectional roots in the period between 1789 and 1865 cannot be treated here. Briefly, the dominant view in the North held that the national government had emerged at the same time as the state governments during the Revolution; that the Union was pemanent unless all parties agreed to its dissolution; and that, under the Constitution, the national government was supreme. By the same token, the dominant view in the South held that the states antedated the national government, which they had created; that the Union was held together by a compact dissolvable by any of the parties to it; and that sovereignty ultimately resided in the states. Both theories are of equal age in the history of American political thought. See Ralph H. Gabriel, *The Course of American Democratic Thought,* 2d ed. (New York: Ronald Press, 1956).

terests (particularly the race issue) and the power to exercise a virtual veto as a section. They maintained this power for nearly a century until its basis was eroded from under them by changing times and situations.

While the southerners were able to frustrate use of these amendments for the protection of individual liberties, from the 1880's to the 1930's the Fourteenth Amendment was used by the United States Supreme Court to restrict state power to regulate private corporations, often over the anguished protests of the states' representatives in Congress. Today, this means of limiting the power of the states has been substantially abandoned by the Court and the states again have wide latitude in the use of their regulatory powers. Instead, the Civil War amendments have been used by the Supreme Court to extend its role as arbiter of the standards of fundamental liberty and criminal justice over state as well as federal law-enforcement agencies.[15]

Though the recent use of these amendments is often denounced as an attempt to increase federal dominion over the states, in fact the Court has acted less to extend federal government authority than to establish its own position as an umpire interested in raising the standards of justice applicable at all levels of government, federal and state alike. Moreover, until recently at least, even where it has appeared to act radically, in virtually every case involving the apparent limitation of the states' powers, the Court's decisions have come only after three-fifths of the states have individually adopted the same positions (at least in theory) on their own initiative. In no important cases except those involving reapportionment have fewer than half the states been on the same side as the Court.[16] This unstated (and

---

[15] For a study of the Court's changing role, see John R. Schmidhauser, *The Supreme Court as Final Arbiter in Federal-State Relations, 1789–1957* (Chapel Hill: University of North Carolina Press, 1958).

[16] Even in the reapportionment cases, nearly half of the state supreme courts had exercised their right of review in reapportionment matters prior to the United States Supreme Court's 1962 rulings. See Advisory Commission on Intergovernmental Relations, *Apportionment of State Legislatures*, December 1962.

perhaps unperceived) "three-fifths rule" can be seen as operative in the whole range of desegregation cases, in the Court's decision to disallow the use of illegally obtained evidence in state courts, in the recently established requirement that counsel be provided in all criminal cases, and in the prohibition of mandatory prayers and Bible-reading in the schools, to name only a few of the "landmark" cases of recent years. It is possible to view these efforts to create more uniform standards as violations of the spirit of federalism which seeks to allow diversity to flourish within the nation, but it is also possible to argue that this unstated three-fifths rule serves to provide an opportunity for adjusting American legal ideas to changes induced by the continuing frontier in a manner consonant with the perpetuation of a dual legal system.

Paradoxically, then, the three Civil War amendments have had a dual effect. They have formally clarified federal supremacy in the written Constitution and have provided the Court with the means to make that supremacy stick in areas previously immune from federal intervention. Yet they also have become the catalysts for the introduction of a modified version of the concurrent majority system into the unwritten constitution for use by both Congress and the Court.

Federalism without Washington

Often unnoticed in discussion of the place of the states in the Federal system is the growing routinization of interstate relationships that are not routed through Washington and which act as a counterbalance to federal activity. The national Constitution does, of course, make reference to interstate relations, setting forth some basic guarantees of "full faith and credit" for state actions of potentially nationwide importance. Still, the practical meaning of those provisions, like those of the rest of the Constitution, have had to be worked out in the political realm.

Three basic forms of routinized interstate relationships have developed. One is the interlocking structure of institutions and professional associations built around the Council of State Governments, ranging from the national and regional Legislative and

Table 16. *Organizations Affiliated with the Council of State Governments, 1964*

Council serves as secretariat for:
Governors' Conference
National Legislative Conference
Conference of Chief Justices
National Association of Attorneys General
National Association of State Budget Officers
National Association of State Purchasing Officials
Parole and Probation Compact Administrators' Association
Association of Juvenile Compact Administrators
National Conference of Government Administrative Officers

Council provides staff services for:
Interstate Conference on Reciprocal Support
Interstate Conference on Water Problems
Conference of Interstate Agencies

Council has cooperative arrangements with:
National Conference of Commissioners on Uniform State Laws
National Conference of State Legislative Leaders

Governors' Conferences to the Association of Juvenile Compact Administrators (see Table 16).[17] The Council of State Governments is a joint governmental agency of all the states, created, supported, and directed by them under the respective laws of each. It defines its functions as assisting in the improvement of state governmental practices, expediting interstate cooperation to solve interstate regional and nationwide problems, and helping to facilitate and improve federal-state relations. Its publicly visible services include conducting conferences on problems of interstate or federal-state concern, undertaking research projects on contemporary governmental problems for one or more states, and, through its various representative assemblies, recommending ap-

[17] The best sources of information about the operations of the Council of State Governments and its affiliated agencies are the council's major publications, *State Government*, published quarterly; *State Government News*, published monthly; and *The Book of the States*, published biennially with a supplement issued in alternate years. See also Brevard Crihfield and Frank Smothers, "The States in the Federal System," *New York University Law Review*, XXXIV, 6 (June 1959), 1018–1036.

propriate courses of action for the states and the federal government to consider in the fields of state government and intergovernmental relations. Much less visible are its activities as a focal point for interstate and federal-state negotiations for the resolution of common problems. These negotiations have covered such diverse topics from coordination of a nationwide civil defense program in World War II to an attempt to negotiate a solution to the Little Rock crisis in 1958 to continuous efforts to adjust federal grant programs to changing state needs.

In the first part of this chapter, we noted how the professional associations, many of which are the council, are more than vehicles for exchanging information and sharing experiences. The exact importance of the leading organization in the group, the Governors' Conference, has been a subject for some discussion in recent years.[18] At the very least, the annual meeting of the governors has become a staging area for political negotiations, often of a magnitude that affects presidential elections. The conference has also provided the states with an additional point of entry into the field of foreign affairs, generally considered the exclusive province of the federal government. This has been done not only by providing another forum for discussion of foreign policy but by contributing to the growing interest of individual governors in becoming active in promoting their states' foreign trade and even in encouraging the states to extend limited technical assistance to underdeveloped nations.

The cities and counties of the United States have their counterpart associations to handle similar problems of mutual interest. The American Municipal Association and the National Association of County Officials speak for the medium-size and smaller cities and the more urbanized counties. The United States Conference of Mayors speaks for the large cities, often in opposition to the associations representing state and county interests, while the National Municipal League speaks for reformers interested in both levels.

[18] See Glenn E. Brooks, *When Governors Convene: The Governors' Conference and National Politics* (Baltimore: Johns Hopkins Press, 1961).

Another form of interstate cooperation is the development of uniform state laws to cover subjects in which nationwide uniformity is desirable but which the states wish to handle without resort to federal legislation. Ninety-two uniform acts and thirty-two model acts have been drafted and submitted to the several states since 1896 when the National Conference of Commissioners on Uniform State Laws submitted the first of them. As of November 15, 1963, three acts dealing with commercial transactions and one providing for reciprocal enforcement of family support laws had been adopted by all fifty states. Five had been adopted by forty-five states or more, all dealing primarily with the administration of justice and inheritance of property. Ten others, covering substantially the same areas, had been adopted by thirty or more states.

Uniform state legislation has received particularly strong support from the nation's commercial interests, as represented by the American Bar Association, which when founded in 1878 initiated the movement. Consequently, most such legislation was related to problems of commerce until recently when other interstate problems in the law enforcement and welfare fields have begun to receive attention. Responsibility for drafting and presenting proposed uniform and model laws is vested in the National Conference of Commissioners on Uniform State Laws, which first met in 1892. Its annual meetings have always been held in connection with those of the ABA and, since 1912, have included representatives from every state. The most important task before the conference in recent years has been the preparation of a Uniform Commercial Code, which has already been adopted by over thirty states. It is designed not only to simplify interstate transactions but to obviate the necessity for increased federal intervention in the field.

The third means for bringing about direct interstate cooperation is through the interstate compact, a constitutionally permitted device that enables two or more states, with the consent of Congress, to enter into an arrangement (in effect, a treaty) for joint action. The most frequently mentioned examples of this arrangement are the Port of New York Authority and the Upper Colorado Basin Compact. The former has long been recognized as a highly successful means by which to handle complex interstate metropolitan transportation problems. The value of the latter for the purpose of ameliorating interstate difficulties was revealed in 1963 when the United States Supreme Court felt it necessary to provide for federal intervention to determine the proper division of water between Arizona and California since the states of the Lower Colorado Basin had been unable to agree on a proper division. Nothing had to be said in that decision about the Upper Basin states' problem, which had been successfully handled through a compact.

The interstate compact was originally devised for regional projects. In recent years, it has been adapted for nationwide use to supplement the system of uniform state laws by providing for mass adherence to uniform standards of administrative action, particularly in the public welfare field. More recently, the interstate compact has become a mechanism for introducing federal participation into regional programs while limiting the extent of federal authority and for involving local governments on a par with state and federal governments at the same time. The Delaware River Basin Compact was the first to do both. Through it, the federal government has been introduced as an equal partner (not a superior) with the states of Delaware, New Jersey, New York, and Pennsylvania as well as the cities of New York and Philadelphia, in the development of solutions of the metropolitan problems of the Delaware River Basin area.

While the compact device to date has been most valuable in the metropolitan Northeast and the arid West, it is rapidly being adapted for use in other parts of the country as well. The new use of the compact device not only indicates the new possibilities for tri-level cooperation to deal with problems of metropolitanization, but also shows how the full range of the intergovernmental sharing system now extends even into the realm of "Federalism without Washington."

CHAPTER SEVEN

The States and Their Civil Communities

There is a clear constitutional difference between the federal-state and the state-local relationship, the former being federal and the latter, unitary. While this difference does have its important effects, it is at least partially reduced through the political process, which gives the localities—particularly the great cities—a strong independent voice of their own. The degree to which the localities acquire or seek to acquire an independent voice varies considerably from state to state, from time to time, and from issue to issue. In every case, the state-local relationship, which is of vital importance within each state's political system, becomes a crucial variable in the state's ability to function as a civil society within the national political system.

In recent years, the federal-state partnership has come to embrace local government in a wider variety of fields than at any time in the past. As a result, some observers have sought to redefine the partnership to include local government as a third element, coequal with the first two. There is some merit in this. Certainly local governments, particularly the big cities, are dealing directly with Washington on a more regular basis than ever before. At the same time, it would be a mistake to think of these direct federal-local relationships as a completely new departure. Just as federal-state collaboration was the norm long before the rise of the so-called "new federalism" of the last generation, so federal-local relations were frequent (relative to the total velocity of government) even in the nineteenth century.[1]

[1] See Daniel J. Elazar, *The American Partnership* (Chicago: University of Chicago Press, 1962), Part Two.

Moreover, the localities and their parent states remain so closely tied together at every point in their relationship that it is hard to separate them from one another for any purpose. When the city of Minneapolis negotiates with the federal Urban Renewal Administration for funds to aid in the redevelopment of part of its central business district that services the economy of Minnesota in many important ways, it is no less an arm of the state than the Livestock Sanitary Board, a state-level agency which cooperates with the federal Department of Agriculture to eradicate cattle diseases in Minnesota's rural areas. Thus, in many respects, direct federal relations with the states' cities are quite similar to direct federal relations with the states' independent departments in their character and overall impact on the states as political systems.[2]

The Constitutional Place of the Cities

Discussion of the constitutional relationship between the fifty states and their local subdivisions (cities and others) is contingent on two fundamental principles. First, in a strictly legal sense it must be understood that all local governments in the United States are creatures of their respective states. The constitutional consequences of this have been stated in Dillon's Rule, framed a half-century ago by one of the nation's leading law writers:

It is a general and undisputed proposition of law that a municipal corporation possesses and can exercise the following powers and no others: First, those granted in express words; second, those necessarily or fairly implied in or incident to the powers expressly granted; third, those essential to the accomplishment of the declared objects and pur-

[2] For example, highway departments in twenty-four states are administratively as independent of state legislative supervision as are cities, having separate governing boards and earmarked revenues. In thirteen more states they are almost as independent. Of course this kind of administrative independence, like municipal home rule, is usually superficial because of the intense involvement of both highway departments and cities in the states' political decision-making processes. See Robert S. Friedman, "State Politics and Highways," Herbert Jacob and Kenneth N. Vines, eds., *Politics in the American States* (Boston: Little, Brown, 1965), Chapter 11.

poses of the corporations—not simply convenient, but indispensable. Any fair, reasonable, substantial doubt concerning the existence of power is resolved by the courts against the corporation, and the power is denied.[3]

Despite the state by state variations in the explicit terms of the legal relationship, this rule is almost invariably construed strictly. The United States Supreme Court has affirmed this relationship, declaring that every local government is "a political subdivision of the state, created as a convenient agency for the exercise of such of the governmental powers of the state as may be intrusted to it." Whatever relations that exist between Washington and the cities must be conducted with this central principle in mind and in force.

This subordinate position of the local governments is clear even in states where local governments exist that were established prior to statehood or even before the state achieved territorial status. It is modified only to the extent that home rule provisions have been written into the constitutions of several states to allow municipal corporations a greater measure of local autonomy. Even in such cases, constitutional home rule has been something less than an effective device to insure the local autonomy anticipated by its proponents. The Colorado constitution, to cite one example, grants all the state's cities with over 2,000 population the right to adopt home rule charters. All cities taking advantage of that right ostensibly gain full power over all local activities, subject to state government intervention only in matters of statewide concern—the most extreme grant of local autonomy possible in the American system. In practice, however, the state legislature has come to regard virtually every significant governmental function undertaken by local government except the actual adoption of the city charter to be of statewide concern, if only because state funds are almost inevitably involved. It has been upheld in

[3] John F. Dillon, *Commentaries on the Law of Municipal Corporations,* 5th ed. (Boston: Little, Brown, 1911), Vol. I, Sec. 237. For a more detailed discussion of the law of municipal corporations by a political scientist, see Charles M. Kneier, *City Government in the United States,* 3d ed. (New York: Harper, 1957).

this interpretation of the constitution by the courts. One effect of this attitude has been to discourage many cities from even going to the trouble of adopting charters.

Colorado is no different than other home rule states. In most, home rule provisions are much less comprehensive, and to the extent that they were designed to provide for local autonomy through a separation of functions, they have ceased to be meaningful. This is certainly not surprising. If federal-state relations cannot be based on a separation of functions because of the existence of universal concerns operating within the same population, how much less is this possible in state-local relations.

Counties and those special districts that do not qualify as municipal corporations under state law are even more restricted in their legal ability to act autonomously even though they may act within broader programmatic limits. The Ohio Supreme Court defined their relative positions over a century ago, when the age of the autonomy-seeking city was just beginning in the United States:

> Municipal corporations proper are called into existence, either at the direct solicitation or by the free consent of the people who compose them. Counties are local subdivisions of a state, created by the sovereign power of the state, of its own sovereign will, without the particular solicitation, consent, or concurrent action of the people who inhabit them. . . .
>
> A municipal corporation proper is created mainly for the interest, advantage, and convenience of the locality and its people; a county organization is created almost exclusively with a view to the policy of the state at large, for purposes of political organization and civil administration, in matters of finance, of education, of provision for the poor . . . of the means of travel and transport, and especially for the general administration of justice.[4]

More recently, there have been many advocates of county home rule, a device widely used today only in California and otherwise still rare even within the great metropolitan states. If extensively adopted, county home rule would give the counties the

---

[4] *Hamilton County* v. *Mighels,* 7 Ohio St. 109 (1857).

same degree of internal autonomy presently available to home rule cities. This will mean internal autonomy to decide which programs to emphasize and how to organize the county for their implementation, but it will not alter the county's essential role as a governmental unit designed to implement state policy nor limit its functional involvement with other levels of government. Indeed, the great increase in county government activity in the last generation, which has led many local government reformers to reconsider the role of the county in a more positive light, is a direct result of the expansion of state and state-federal programs that must be administered locally. Furthermore, the counties' dependence upon state aid (which is usually greater than that of any other general local government) tends to cement the position of the county as an arm of the state.

Home rule, then, is actually a grant of institutional autonomy that enables local governments to "sit in on the game" of intergovernmental functional collaboration holding a potentially better hand than they might were they more thoroughly dependent upon their states for institutional reorganization. As such, it is a useful staring point from which to develop meaningful local autonomy but it is no guarantor of that autonomy itself.

There is one important constitutional bulwark that protects the political status of local communities by protecting the existence of their essential governmental institutions. In the largest constitutional sense, given the realities of politics, no general purpose local government, not even those legally least autonomous, can be abolished by the state without the consent of its voting residents. This guarantee, whether written into the state's fundamental law (as it often is) or not, exists by virtue of the state political system itself. No state legislature is likely to act to abolish a city, county, or township without first obtaining clear local consent. As reformers seeking metropolitan area consolidation or rural county reorganization have repeatedly discovered, local publics of every type are of one mind in resisting this kind of constitutional change. This guarantee, then, is almost universally an ironclad bulwark of local efforts to maintain institutional autonomy though it does nothing directly to aid functional autonomy.

The Civil Community

While local autonomy by charter, in the manner proposed by advocates of home rule, is clearly limited, the weaknesses of constitutional decentralization do not preclude the development of substantial local autonomy through the political process. Indeed, even in those states with no constitutional provisions for home rule, local governments often gain the equivalent in autonomy through their ability to carve important niches for themselves in the structure of state politics. So it is in Illinois where cities have no power to adopt home rule charters but can choose any of the standard options of municipal government structure in use in the United States today (the mayor-alderman, council-manager, or commission forms of government; city councils elected by district or at large, or a combination of the two). Students of Illinois politics know that cities in that state have as great a measure of actual autonomy as do cities in Colorado.

The Illinois case is typical. Constitutionally dependent upon their states for their very existence, local communities are at the same time protected by the same political diffusion of power that protects the position of the states vis-à-vis the federal government. Most of them—particularly the larger cities—have been able to use their political power to secure a measure of autonomy not formally theirs under constitutional law. This has given them a measure of control over all government activities within their limits regardless of the level of government formally responsible for them.

This is possible because local communities may also become political systems. Local political systems are not organized within the compass of a single overarching government as are those of states and the nation nor are they as comprehensive and complex, except in the case of the largest cities. Their structure is based on the semiformal interrelationships of numerous local governments:

cities, counties, townships, school districts, and special purpose districts. In reality, then, it is possible to speak of "cities" as political systems only in the case of the five to ten very largest ones whose city governments come close to being overarching. In every other case, the term is but marginally useful as a shorthand definition of a more complex political order. In most of those cases, it may be so marginal that it is actually misleading.

A better term to describe the complex of governments and quasi-governments quartered locally that serve a given locality is the "civil community." We may define a local political system as the organized sum of the political institutions which function in a given locality to provide the bundle of governmental services and activities which can be manipulated locally to serve local needs in light of the local value system. Accordingly the entity a local political system serves becomes a community insofar as it is organized for political—or civil—purposes. Such an entity can properly be called a civil community—a smaller counterpart of the civil society designed to serve the immediate communal ends of people who live in more or less immediate proximity to one another. The politically significant components of the civil community include (1) the formally established local governments serving it, such as the municipal governments, the county, the school districts, and the like; (2) the local agencies of the state and federal governments insofar as they are adjuncts of the local community existing primarily to serve it, such as the local branches of the state employment office and the post office; (3) the public nongovernmental bodies serving local governmental or quasi-governmental purposes, such as the chamber of commerce and the community welfare council; (4) the political parties or factions functioning within the civil community to organize political competition; (5) the system of interest groups functioning in the local political area to represent the various local interests; and (6) the body of written constitutional material and unwritten tradition serving as a framework within which sanctioned political action must take place and as a check against unsanctioned political behavior.

The civil community as a political system is a much more powerful—and hence more autonomous—entity than any single local government. Even though the civil community has no formal status in law, it has carved a place for itself in the constitutional system that is just now coming to be recognized and has yet to be precisely defined. Its position is based on the ability of the formally disjointed governmental elements within its limits to satisfy local needs (at least minimally) by mobilizing local and outside support in a manner that conforms to the dominant sentiments of the community.

Federalism and the Civil Community

As one focal point within the national system of systems, the civil community serves in five major capacities: as acquirer of outside aids—governmental and nongovernmental—for local needs; as an adapter of government actions and services to local values and conditions; as an experimenter with new functions and services (or readaptions of traditional ones); as initiator of governmental programs of particular relevance locally that may or may not later become widespread; and as the means by which a local aggregation of people can secure an effective voice in state and national governmental decisions affecting them.[5]

It should be apparent that the intergovernmental dimension is of the essence in forming, shaping, and marking the limits of the civil community. Moreover, it is in its relationships with the state and federal governments that the shape of the civil community is best revealed. In a system whose governments are all highly intermeshed, every civil community from the greatest to the smallest has extensive and pervasive relations with its state and with the federal government. Indeed, its role is to serve as the means for transmitting many of the services provided by those governments to their citizens, adding appropriate local

[5] This is discussed in greater detail in Daniel J. Elazar, "Local Government in Intergovernmental Perspective," in Lois Pelekoudis, ed., *Illinois Local Government* (Urbana: University of Illinois, 1960).

adaptations. The following example, while presenting the sharing system in its most extreme form, points up the extent to which routinized intergovernmental sharing has penetrated into every corner of American civic life and the way in which the civil community exists to bring some sense of order into the chaos of collaboration.

Somewhere, in every organized county in the United States, is a public health official whose official title is "sanitarian." Sometimes he is employed by the county itself, sometimes by the major city in the county, sometimes by a regional health department. The santitarian, an office created as a product of a formal co-operative program, provides an excellent, if extreme, example of the intermeshing of federal, state, and local functions from the perspective of the public servant. Look at the sanitarian in Arkansas' Saline County, population 25,000. He is appointed by the state under merit standards established by the federal government in collaboration with the professional associations of public health administrators. Most of his salary as sanitarian comes from state and federal funds but it is supplemented by the largest city in the county which pays him for his services as city plumbing inspector. His office and its equipment are supplied by the county, with an assist from the city, and part of his expenses are paid from county funds.

His day to day operations are equally intermingled. He carries out his task of enforcing the pure food and drug laws under federal standards, though he enforces state law when inspecting commodities that have not been in interstate commerce. To make the system more complex, he inspects milk coming into the county from another state as a local official operating under authority granted him by his state. He acts as a federal officer when he impounds impure drugs imported from a neighboring state, a federal-state officer when he distributes typhoid immunization serum, a state officer when he enforces standards of industrial hygiene, a state-county officer when he inspects the purity of his city's water supply, and he completes the roll as a city officer when he compels the city butchers to adopt more hygienic methods of handling their garbage. To cover any situations not otherwise provided for in his other mandates, he is a deputy sheriff and an ex officio member of the city police force.

It is apparent that the sanitarian is responsible for all public health and sanitation business in his own county. He considers all such business his business and does not stop, in the course of his work, to consider which hat he is wearing at that particular time unless he is forced to.

In counties containing larger urban communities, health departments are frequently autonomous governments under the law and in the largest communities are relatively large and complex departments of the city or county government with specialists available to handle the divergent tasks confronting our lone sanitarian, but the spread of concerns remains as involved. Greater resources and larger staffs enhance the possibilities for local decision-making by providing local sources of expertise that make state and federal "interference" less necessary. At the same time, the larger local programs increase their communities' involvement in the overall system through more intensive activities financed by larger federal and state grants, the sponsorship of "pilot projects" and the like.

Local communities are intermeshed with the state and federal governments many ways and for many purposes. City officials seek expert advice on building a jail; park commissioners seek financial aid in developing a local recreational facility; local businessmen seek funds for airport improvement and for transfer of an old military installation to their city; public and private parties seek the right to issue bonds for industrial development and seek grants of fire-fighting equipment under the civil defense program. All require outside assistance, and assistance for all but the last two items can be acquired from either level of government depending upon which is most convenient. It is a massive task just to list the aids and services available to the civil community—from model plumbing codes to construction of marinas to disaster relief. And these activities, even the federal ones, are not viewed locally as a forcible intrusion of a distant government but almost invariably as the successful consequence of local activity in obtaining federal and state programs to serve local ends in a manner good for community, state, and nation. This local view, developed over time by concrete experiences rather than by abstract logic, is historically the correct one. Because the federal principle of noncentralization extends down to the local level, even outside contributions—financial, technical, or political—can be assimilated and managed locally for local ends. If the system appears on the surface to be mildly chaotic, this does not mean that some order does not exist within its bounds. While every government level may be involved in all governmental activities, each operates from its own position of power and together they provide a series of focal points for the organization of the system.

The Civil Community and the State

Highly important in all this is the continuing close connection between the state and its local subdivisions. Let us return to our exemplary and apparently overdivided sanitarian. His apparent fragmentation is useful to the political analyst attempting to understand the federal system as it operates, but with all the hats he may wear from time to time, he remains, first and foremost, a local official appointed by an arm of his state to serve a specific community by handling its public health needs. His formal place and informal ties revolve around his location within and attachment to the civil community he serves. While his office is charged with certain basic federal responsibilities (in a strict sense, he is never a federal officer except insofar as he is mandated by the state to enforce federal laws), the final range of his activities is determined by his state and local community.

Three central factors aid the localities in their ability to exercise substantial control over the bundle of governmental services and activities provided locally, regardless of their formal point of origin. In the first place, the localities which do exercise control at any level of significance do so because they have organized as civil communities. It is the ability of the local health department to (1) draw upon the fiscal resources of local governments it serves to support its continuing activities and to serve as "bait" to attract outside funds, (2) utilize the political skills of the local delegation in the state legislature and the region's congressman, (3) mobilize influentials in the community through a community welfare council or the like to support its plans, (4) convince voters of its value through services rendered and thus gain a constituency that will support it in its relations with the local governing bodies, and (5) share its range of interests with the public nongovernmental agencies concerned with public health within the civil community (such as the hospitals and the anti-disease associations) that makes it possible for it to shape its programs to meet local needs no matter what the sources of their support. All the foregoing reflect the set of interacting institutions and relationships within a given locality that go to make up a civil community.

The ability of the civil community to exercise control over the bundle of governmental activities and services within its boundaries depends upon the extent to which it is organized to exercise that control. The lonesome sanitarian in the small Arkansas county is kept so busy performing functions of state and federal origin that he is hardly in any position to develop a community health policy and to implement it. A larger county health department—such as that of Peoria, Illinois (population 190,000), with its public health nursing staff of nine; its sanitarian staff of four; its two public health educators, dental director, business administrator, and its full-time director of health—an M.D.—can not only provide a full range of services at the minimum level demanded by state law and national standards, but can develop additional programs to serve specific local needs or experiment with new programs in fields not yet covered by state and federal policy. It can do all this only with outside financial assistance but it assimilates that assistance within the framework of a community health policy developed within the civil community. Thus professionalization and bureaucratization within the civil community can enhance its position vis-à-vis the professionals and bureaucrats of both the state and federal governments.

Finally, the ability of the civil community to control the bundle of governmental services and activities within its boundaries is enhanced by its position within its state's civil society. In confronting the national pressures evident in everything that concerns it, the civil community is strengthened by its position as part of a civil society which is subnational in scope and accordingly has interests which not only need not be identical with national interests but which can even go counter to them; which is concerned with its own subdivisions to a substantial degree; and which also is large enough and strong enough within the national civil society to take appropriate action to successfully defend its own concerns and those of its component civil communities, where necessary.

The value of the state civil society to the civil community is apparent in several ways. There is the already noted ability of the state to mobilize its congressional delegation to run political interference for the legitimate (and sometimes not so legitimate) interests of its civil communities in matters involving federal action. Every state has a well-developed bureaucracy which tends to be more professionalized the more it is involved in cooperative programs. Insofar as that bureaucracy is able to shape federal programs along the lines it deems most appropriate for the state it serves, it is in a position to either help a local bureaucracy tailor those programs to better fit its civil community or to provide the same assistance for civil communities too small to have local bureaucracies of their own. The better state governments not only provide a shield for localities in their relationship with the federal government but also provide technical and political support for aggressive local governments that wish to lead the way in negotiating specific new programs with their federal counterparts.

It is true that for these benefits, the state exacts its price. Most civil communities must compete for attention from their states before they can hope to obtain federal assistance. Securing state attention may depend on many factors, including those of partisan politics not immediately relevant to the issue at hand. The more energetic states, which run the best interference, also tend to exert the most control over local use of federal aids while the least energetic states actually jeopardize their civil communities' chances to get federal assistance, since the federal system is so constructed as to make state action almost mandatory before all but the largest localities can get a proper hearing.

The role of the states is particularly important in the case of medium-size and smaller civil communities, which do not have the political power necessary to gain direct access to Washington by themselves. These communities—which contain the bulk of the nation's population—benefit most from association with their states. In most cases, their policies tend to be reasonably similar to the policies of their states and their needs can best be satisfied with state assistance. Not only that but as components of the state civil societies whose leadership, political and professional, can and usually does have face to face contact with their opposite numbers at the state level, they can also influence state policies, generally even more than they can hope to influence national ones.

The Great Metropolitan Centers: A Special Case

The largest metropolitan centers, the so-called "big city bloc," do possess the political power needed to go directly to Washington. They, in turn, often feel frustrated by their states' insistence on controlling their access as well, just as they anger the state leadership when they seek to maintain their direct channels to the federal government. This mutual frustration is heightened when state policies differ from those of the big cities. For, in the last analysis, the states do not exist just to run interference for their civil communities. They have policies and interests of their own to which the civil communities must bend, ones that frequently reflect values quite different from those of the metropolis. At the same time, the great metropolitan centers also have policies and interests of their own which are equally demanding because they emerge from entities as complex and internally self-sufficient as are the states themselves.

The very largest metropolitan areas in the country, the eight with populations in excess of two million within a single state (Table 17), have become virtually self-contained civil societies in their own right. They contain sufficient political variety and governmental complexity to rival the state civil societies in which they are located. For them, their respective states have had to create special constitutional arrangements unlike those prevailing in connection with lesser urban communities. Frank J. Goodnow noted this phenomenon as early as 1897 when he commented that the metropolitan city (his term) "will be more generally than in the case with smaller cities entrusted with the discharge of functions of the Federal and State governments . . . The Metropoli-

Table 17. The Metropolitan Civil Societies, 1960 *

METROPOL-ITAN AREA	POPULATION	LAND AREA, SQUARE MILES	NUMBER OF LOCAL GOVERN-MENTS	NUMBER OF CITIES WITH POPULATION OVER 50,000	NUMBER OF CITIES WITH POPULATION 25,000–49,999
New York	10,694,633	2,149	555	5	5
Los Angeles	6,742,696	4,842	348	20	25
Chicago	6,220,913	3,714	1,060	9	13
Oakland/San Francisco	3,762,360	1,965	241	9	14
Philadelphia a	3,591,523	2,180	700	2	2
Detroit	2,783,359	3,313	398	9	8
Boston	2,589,301	969	125	9	8
Pittsburgh	2,405,435	3,051	806	1	4

a Includes area in Pennsylvania only.

* Prepared from U.S. Census data.

tan City . . . has grown from many centers [and] is thus in many cases a state in miniature." [6]

While it is entirely possible to establish detailed objective criteria that identify, define, and delimit metropolitan civil societies, the existence of this type of metropolitan entity is equally apparent from common sense observation. Those great cities whose spokesmen take the lead in publicly objecting to "state domination of cities" or in complaining about "inadequate state concern for urban problems" can be easily identified as the centers of metropolitan regions that encompass from 1,000 to 5,000 square miles and contain from 125 to 1,060 separate local governments including from 4 to 45 cities of 25,000 population or more. These are the cities that come to mind when the mass media refer to the misnamed "urban-rural conflict." They are the cities whose mayors dominate the United States Conference of Mayors and who are public figures of some national importance in their own right, usually rivaling their states' governors as centers of attention.

The special cases presented by these metropolitan civil societies have, to some extent, been formally recognized by their states. Most of the states have written into their constitutions specific provisions governing the special character of their great cities. Indeed, there appears to be a substantial relationship between the time such constitutional provisions were first incorporated into the state's fundamental law and the achievement of a population of approximately two million by the metropolis in question. Chicago is a case in point. In 1904, Illinois voters approved a change in the state's 1870 constitution allowing Chicago to adopt a special charter by local option, a right not available to any other city in the state, and effectively making the legislature a separate constituent assembly for the city. The census of 1900 showed Chicago's population to be 1,932,000, enough to qualify it for designation as a "civil society" under the terms suggested here.

Furthermore, every one of the states in which these metro-

[6] Frank J. Goodnow, *Municipal Problems* (New York: Century Co., 1897).

politan centers are located has made some special provision for handling the specialized problems of its metropolis beyond any constitutional recognition of its uniqueness. These include such devices as separate legislative commissions to handle legislation for the metropolis at the state level in Illinois; strong county home rule in Los Angeles County; and the Massachusetts Metropolitan District Commission which operates greater Boston's sewer, water, and park systems and the Metropolitan Transit Authority which operates the transit system, both of which are under the direct control of the state in personnel and budgetary matters.[7]

Without elaborating further on this theme, it is apparent that the great metropolitan centers do stand in a unique position within the structure of American federalism. Neither states nor ever likely to become states, they are not simply local subdivisions of their states as the notion is generally understood. For better or worse, Congress and the state legislatures have recognized their anomalous position by providing for direct federal-city relations in the programs that affect them, primarily in the areas of public housing, urban redevelopment, and airport construction. More recently, the antipoverty programs, which will have their greatest impact in the larger cities, have also been routed to them directly.

The Fiscal Pattern

While the character of sharing is not necessarily shaped by the pattern of intergovernmental expenditure and the impacts of intergovernmental relations are often independent of the amount of money involved, the fiscal situation does tell us something about the relative roles of the state and federal governments

[7] Several of these relationships are mentioned, albeit disapprovingly, in Kneier, *op. cit.*, Chapter 4. Others are discussed in Edward C. Banfield, ed., *Urban Government* (New York: Free Press, 1961), Part II. It should be noted that these separate arrangements were not always introduced to formalize a new relationship. In Massachusetts and Missouri, for example, they were introduced as a result of conflict between old and new elites.

in aiding the civil community. In 1960, the states transferred some $9.3 billion to their local subdivisions in contrast to direct federal aid to localities of $642 million (out of a total of $7 billion transferred to the states and localities combined). State aids to localities were primarily for education, highways, and public welfare, as was federal aid to the states. Direct federal aid to the localities went primarily for education and housing and community development programs. In the first, the federal expenditure of $245 million represented less than 5 per cent of the total state aid to localities but in the second, the federal expenditure of $226 million was nearly ten times greater than that of the states.[8]

Since 1960, the amount of direct federal aid to localities has increased but the relative proportions have not changed significantly for the regular programs. With the introduction of special federal aids for area redevelopment and combating poverty, the overall percentage of direct federal aid to the localities is increasing. Moreover, the role of the states in the aid pattern has been altered in those programs. In the established fields of governmental activity, federal money often reaches the localities after going via the states, as in the case of the public welfare programs. Indeed, most federal funds are not even recognized as such by the local authorities handling them since they are submerged in state money. In the new programs, however, the states participate as advisers, planners, and coordinators to the extent that they wish to do so but often do not handle the funds directly.

Variations in State-Local Relations

While it is possible to describe generally the place of the civil community in the federal system, there are important state by state variations in the politics of state-local (and hence federal-state-local) relations. These variations are based on the same factors that influence state-federal relations, particularly sectionalism

[8] Data from U.S. Bureau of the Census, *Governmental Finances in 1960.*

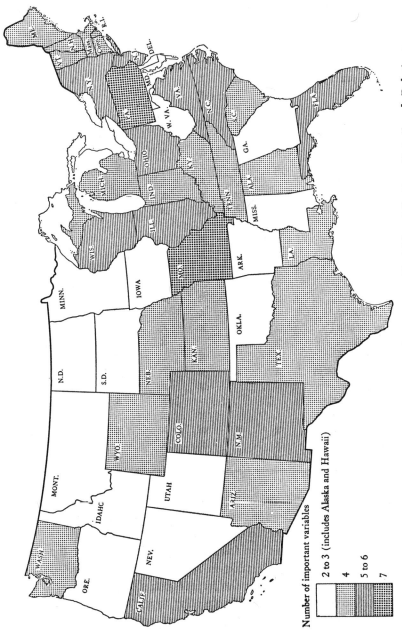

FIGURE 7. State by State Distribution of Important Variables Affecting State-Local Relations

Number of important variables

2 to 3 (includes Alaska and Hawaii)

4

5 to 6

7

Table 18. Important Variables in State-Local Political Conflict, by State

	1	2	3	4	5	6	7
Alabama		x	x	x		x	
Alaska		x	x				
Arizona	x	x	x				x
Arkansas		x	x	x			
California	x		x		x	x	x
Colorado	x	x	x	x	x		
Connecticut	x	x	x		x		
Delaware			x	x			
Florida	x	x	x	x		x	
Georgia	x		x	x			
Hawaii		x				x	
Idaho	x	x	x				
Illinois	x	x	x		x		x
Indiana	x	x	x	x			
Iowa	x			x		x	
Kansas	x	x	x	x			
Kentucky		x	x	x		x	
Louisiana		x	x	x		x	
Maine	x	x		x		x	
Maryland		x			x		
Massachusetts	x	x	x		x		
Michigan		x	x	x			x
Minnesota			x	x			
Mississippi		x	x		x		
Missouri	x	x	x	x	x	x	x
Montana	x		x	x			
Nebraska	x		x	x	x		

and political culture, but are also heavily influenced by such factors as urbanization and metropolitanization that are less important as variables in the larger national pattern.

If hard data on the influence of these factors at the state level is scarce, the situation in regard to state-local relations is even worse. Allowing for the imperfections of the data, it is still possible to construct a table showing in a general way the most important influences on the state-local political relationships in each of the fifty states. Table 18 presents seven factors that are

Variations in State-Local Relations

	1	2	3	4	5	6	7
Nevada			x				x
New Hampshire	x	x		x	x		
New Jersey	x	x	x		x		x
New Mexico	x	x		x		x	x
New York	x	x	x	x	x		x
North Carolina	x	x	x	x			x
North Dakota			x	x			
Ohio	x	x	x	x	x		x
Oklahoma			x	x			x
Oregon			x		x		
Pennsylvania	x	x	x	x	x	x	x
Rhode Island	x	x			x		
South Carolina		x	x	x		x	
South Dakota	x		x	x			
Tennessee		x	x	x	x		
Texas		x	x	x	x		x
Utah	x	x		x			
Vermont	x	x		x		x	
Virginia	x	x	x	x	x		x
Washington	x		x		x		x
West Virginia				x		x	
Wisconsin	x	x	x	x	x	x	
Wyoming	x	x	x	x			
	(31)	(33)	(40)	(36)	(22)	(16)	(16)

KEY: 1: Political Culture   4: Urban-Rural
      2: General Culture   5: Metropolitan-Nonmetropolitan
      3: Sectionalism   6: Localism
                 7: Intermetropolitan

important influences on those relationships and Figure 7 shows their state by state distribution.

Some states quite clearly have more variables influencing the state-local relationship than others. Since the question of intensity of influence must remain open, the most that can be done on the table is to indicate the existence of each variable as a visible influence. All things being equal, we might well expect a higher degree of state-local conflict where there are more variables. However, we do not know if all things are equal. In some states a few influential variables are so important that they provoke intense conflict while in others, the many weak variables counterbalance one another to lessen conflict.

There is some evidence that those states with more active variables do less governmentally to help their civil communities than their sisters; that is, the variety of conflicts or potential conflicts tends to prevent the states from acting as units to solve local problems. There is evidence that this is true in Illinois, Missouri, New Jersey, Ohio, and Virginia. The New York and Colorado situations certainly stand as exceptions to this. While the case is not proven either way in Florida, New Mexico, and Pennsylvania, the evidence in all three cases points in the direction of the first alternative.

Diversity of political cultures is a potent influence on the state-local relationship in thirty-one states. As already indicated, cities frequently represent aggregations of population harboring political cultures that differ from the aggregations living in the surrounding areas. It is quite likely (one might say almost certain) that in every state there are a few cities, dominated by a political culture alien to that of the state as a whole, which will come into conflict with the state on a variety of issues. The entire question is greatly aggravated when a state itself is divided among two political cultures whereby the cities of the minority political culture must champion a sectional as well as a local interest against state officials at least dimly aware that there are fundamental differences of interest involved.

General cultural differences are here defined rather loosely, ranging from the differences between the French-Canadians and Yankees in New England to the differences between the mountain people and the lowlanders in the southern states. Among the specific differences recognized in Table 18 are:

"Rednecks"—Lowlanders (Alabama, Florida, Mississippi, South Carolina)
"Hillbillies"—Lowlanders (Arkansas, Kentucky, North Carolina, Tennessee)
White Men—Eskimos/Indians (Alaska, Arizona)

Variations in State-Local Relations

"Anglos"—"Mexicans" (Arizona, Colorado, New Mexico, Texas)
"Anglos"—Orientals (Hawaii)
"Gentiles"—Mormons (Arizona, Idaho, Utah, Wyoming)
Yankees—Southerners (Illinois, Kansas, Missouri, Ohio)
Old Immigrants—New Immigrants (Connecticut, Illinois, Maine, New Jersey, New York, Pennsylvania, Rhode Island)
Anglo-Protestants—French Catholics (Louisiana, New Hampshire, Vermont)
Protestants—Catholics (Wisconsin)

Thirty-three states have some form of general cultural cleavage of greater or lesser intensity.

Intrastate sectionalism is the most widespread variable of all, found in forty states. Sectionalism differs from localism in that the sectional struggle is oriented toward a distribution of state benefits or allocation of state governmental power among different parts of the state while localism reflects a desire on the part of specific localities to have little or nothing to do with the state. Sectionalism is a phenomenon found in both culturally homogeneous and culturally heterogeneous states while localism usually indicates a cultural difference which the locals feel can only be protected by pursuing a policy of isolationism. This kind of localism is found in sixteen states though in some, like Iowa and Vermont, it is not so much an active isolationism as a vestige of earlier notions of local autonomy.

The urban-rural cleavage refers specifically to conflicts between urban and rural (including urban county seats in rural counties) areas. While this cleavage still exists in thirty-six states, it is of diminishing importance outside the South, the Great Plains, and northern New England where the tide of urbanization is still flowing in. In its place a metropolitan-nonmetropolitan cleavage has developed, embracing urban dwellers on both sides who have different perspectives on the urban situation. This is likely to be one of the great cleavages of the future whose full meaning is not yet apparent. Today it exists in twenty-two states. A variation of this is the cleavage between metropolitan areas, which develops as a result of conflicting immediate interests or a conflict of traditional cultures or both. Such cleavages exist in sixteen states. All told, twenty-seven states have some sort of intraurban cleavage that is replacing or already has replaced the older urban-rural cleavage.

The national pattern of state distribution of the seven variables is also significant (see Figure 7). Though the variables of urbanization and metropolitanization are included within the seven, they do not appear to be the most important elements in determining the extent to which a state has more or fewer active points of cleavage. Instead, geographic location appears to be of central importance. Those states that straddle the socio-cultural middle of the country, particularly those east of the Mississippi which cover the nation's main-traveled routes, plus those along the east coast which have the longest histories and have been affected by the most trends and currents, have more cleavages than any others. This is so even when the variables are held constant. The two states with the most cleavages, Pennsylvania and Missouri, are located at particularly critical crossroads in the overall national pattern. Those states off the beaten path have the fewest cleavages. The parallels between this distribution and the distribution of political cultures are striking.

Traditions of Centralism and Localism

One more element must be added to this consideration of the state-local political struggle. Some states have traditions of internal centralism while others traditionally encourage localism (Figure 8).

New England has a localistic tradition dating back to its settlement while the South has an equally ancient tradition of centralized state government. In the former section, those states which have escaped the most intense pressures of social change in the past century have retained this localistic tradition. Consequently, their state governments assume as little responsibility as possible and leave most of the burden of government to their local subdivisions. In the other New England states and in those newer states dominated by Yankee settlers, localism has been

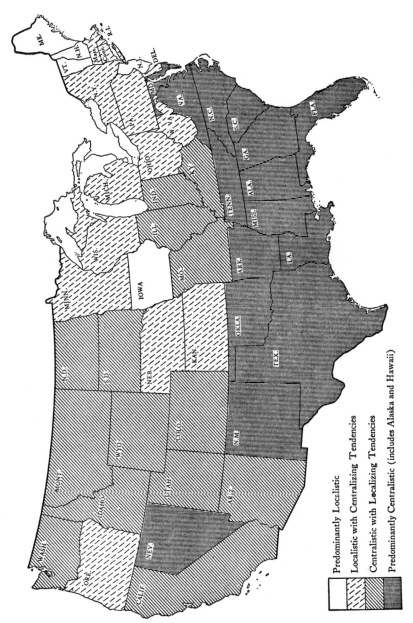

FIGURE 8. State Traditions of Centralism-Localism

Predominantly Localistic

Localistic with Centralizing Tendencies

Centralistic with Localizing Tendencies

Predominantly Centralistic (includes Alaska and Hawaii)

modified by a degree of centralization brought about by a desire to raise the standards of state services coupled with a recognition that this had to be done under direction from the state level. In these states, the pattern has been to involve the state governments where necessary while allowing the greatest feasible amount of local discretion and control at all times.

The southern states never relinquished their centralized controls over their subdivisions but neither have they used them to expand government activities at the state level. Southern state government remains nominally centralized and minimally active. Those states of the Ohio and Mississippi valleys settled initially by southerners but subsequently influenced by Yankees modified their centralist tendencies to add an infusion of localism. Over the years, they have tended to decentralize government activities and even the power of decision-making.

Localism has persisted in the middle states longer than elsewhere because of the high levels of internal cleavage in those states, particularly cleavage in the matter of political culture which would dictate what government should or should not do, how much of its resources should be devoted to doing it, and how it should be done. Where there has been little statewide agreement on these questions in program after program, it has often proved easier to simply allow the various local subdivisions of the state to handle them after the fashion of local desires and under minimum state standards.

In general, the northern states west of the Mississippi were settled after the era of extreme localism had passed. The demands of the new technology of the latter half of the nineteenth century were in themselves enough to require strong state governments from the first. Consequently, with the exceptions of states like Iowa and Oregon whose governmental patterns were established before the end of the era of localism, government in those states was strong at the center from the beginning but even in them there was strong pressure on behalf of localism, leading to the development of a policy of substantial decentralization within an internal sharing system.

Federal aid has played its role in strengthening state governments at least since the mid-nineteenth century. Federal grants to the states, including land grants, caused state governments to assume greater power and develop more comprehensive governing mechanisms to distribute that aid properly. Here, too, the states' role as political systems has been important. At first, the federal government channeled its aid to specific localities with the states functioning in purely ministerial capacities to handle the transfers. After it was demonstrated that this system was wasteful of resources, administratively inefficient, and politically disruptive, the states and Congress altered the system to channel most federal aid to the states where the decisions for local distribution could be made on a more comprehensive and controlled basis. By 1850, this transformation had taken place and the states benefiting from federal aid began to use that aid to strengthen their own governmental structures—a tradition that has continued ever since.[9]

While centralization has affected all states, there has been a strong tendency for the original set of attitudes toward centralism and localism to remain as powerful influences within each individual state. Localities adjust their demands implicitly to the state's tradition if only because they know that the tradition will generally dictate the maximum they can expect to get.

The relationships between state and local expenditures for schools and public welfare throw some light on the various patterns of centralism-localism. Some care must be taken in drawing conclusions based on expenditure patterns because—as we know in the case of federal-state expenditures—a high proportion of state expenditure may be accompanied by a high degree of local control because of the nature of the state's political system. To some extent, the reverse is also true; relatively high local expenditures may still be accompanied by close state control over local programs. Moreover, differences in patterns of sectionalism and political culture attach different meanings to the same apparent levels of expenditure.

The relative proportions of state and local school expenditures have changed very little over the years since the late nine-

[9] For a discussion of this, see Elazar, *op. cit.*

teenth century.[10] In the New England states, which pioneered the public schools, local responsibility has been pronounced ever since the beginning of public support for education. The New England pattern was spread wherever the Yankees migrated,

Table 19. *Per Capita State School Expenditures in Relation to Local School Expenditures, 1961* [a]

HIGH (22)	PROPORTIONATE (6)	LOW (20)
Minnesota (LC)	California (CL)	Arizona (CL)
Nevada (C)	Michigan (LC)	Oregon (LC)
New York (LC)	Connecticut (LC)	Colorado (CL)
Utah (CL)	Idaho (CL)	Montana (CL)
Wyoming (CL)	Rhode Island (LC)	North Dakota (CL)
New Mexico (C)	Virginia (C)	Indiana (CL)
Washington (CL)		Maryland (CL)
Alabama (C)		Vermont (L)
Delaware (LC)		Iowa (L)
Georgia (C)		Wisconsin (LC)
Louisiana (C)		Nebraska (LC)
Oklahoma (C)		New Jersey (L)
Pennsylvania (LC)		South Dakota (CL)
Texas (C)		Kansas (LC)
Florida (C)		Illinois (CL)
West Virginia (LC)		Massachusetts (LC)
North Carolina (C)		Ohio (LC)
Mississippi (C)		Maine (L)
South Carolina (C)		Missouri (CL)
Tennessee (C)		New Hampshire (L)
Arkansas (C)		
Kentucky (CL)		

KEY: C: Centralism predominates
CL: Mixed centralist and localist tendencies
L: Localism predominates

[a] Alaska and Hawaii omitted for lack of data.
Rankings based on National Education Association, *Rankings of the States, 1963.*

[10] Paul Mort, Walter Reusser, and John Polby, *Public School Finance,* 3d ed. (New York: McGraw-Hill, 1960), indicates that "the position of the several states in regard to state support had already become fairly well fixed by 1890" (p. 197).

though west of the Mississippi, conditions made it necessary for the states to assume a greater role in financing local school districts. In the southern states, on the other hand, effective public education systems did not come into existence until the post-Civil War period when they were instituted on a statewide basis by Yankee carpetbaggers in control of the states in question. Southern local governments were neither eager nor financially able to assume the burden of public support for education and southern tradition favored state-centered leadership in any case. In the middle states, the pattern of state as against local expenditures was established after political conflict between the two schools of thought.

The consequences of these variations are apparent in the rankings of the states by the National Education Association in terms of proportionate state and local expenditures for schools (Table 19). The states with the highest proportionate state expenditures are either (1) those with strong traditions of centralization or (2) those with centralized administrative structures or budgetary patterns that overlay traditions of decentralization. All but one of the states with proportionate state and local expenditures are influenced by the moralistic political culture and also have strong traditions of activism at the local level, leading to a closer sharing of fiscal responsibility. At the low end of the range, the states are either those leaning toward localism or the larger states of the Northwest which have relatively little state revenue to allocate to their local subdivisions.[11]

A similar pattern is observable in the public welfare field (Table 20). Most of the centralized states of the South and several of the southwestern states where centralization is really stronger than the localistic tendencies require their local governments to contribute less than 5 per cent of the total state-local expenditure for public welfare. At the other end of the scale, the wealthier states that spend more for welfare at both the state and

[11] For further discussion of state patterns in education, see Robert H. Salisbury, "State Politics and Education" in Jacob and Vines, *op. cit.*, Chapter 9.

Table 20. Percentage of Total Public Welfare Expenditures by State and Local Governments, 1961 [a] [b]

	PERCENTAGE STATE	PERCENTAGE LOCAL
Washington	60.1	0.0
Pennsylvania	54.9	0.0
Utah	45.0	0.0
Louisiana	35.1	0.0
Arkansas	26.8	0.0
Arizona	32.9	0.1
Alabama	25.9	0.1
Missouri	35.8	0.2
Idaho	37.1	0.3
New Mexico	31.7	0.4
Oklahoma	38.4	0.7
Mississippi	22.4	0.7
South Carolina	25.6	0.9
Kentucky	25.3	1.4
Texas	27.5	1.6
West Virginia	24.6	2.1
Florida	26.9	4.5
Tennessee	20.0	5.1
Rhode Island	50.6	5.2
Georgia	22.0	5.2
Illinois	55.8	6.8
Connecticut	58.4	7.6
Ohio	49.5	8.1
Colorado	48.6	8.7
Maine	27.9	10.1
Vermont	23.5	10.5

local levels, plus the centralized states with strong localistic tendencies of the Northwest, have the highest proportions of local expenditure for welfare.[12] The most rural of the states with localistic tendencies and moralistic political cultures are grouped in the middle, a position possibly indicating their reliance upon

[12] Pennsylvania is one of the interesting exceptions in both the educational and public welfare fields. A state with many internal cleavages and a strong localistic tradition, it has used its authority as a state to collect funds without centralizing a commensurate level of power over the programs it supports. This policy has actually served to help overcome the strong tend-

Traditions of Centralism and Localism

	PERCENTAGE STATE	PERCENTAGE LOCAL
Nebraska	27.6	11.5
South Dakota	25.8	12.3
North Dakota	35.8	12.8
Oregon	40.1	14.4
Maryland	26.3	14.6
Virginia	15.7	15.2
Iowa	31.6	15.8
North Carolina	11.9	17.0
California	38.0	19.9
Delaware	33.1	20.1
Kansas	24.7	22.0
Massachusetts	36.2	23.7
New Hampshire	24.0	25.7
Michigan	36.2	27.1
New York	32.0	30.4
Indiana	17.2	30.7
Nevada	25.2	32.2
Montana	21.7	32.4
Wyoming	19.7	32.4
Wisconsin	24.8	32.5
New Jersey	29.2	33.0
Minnesota	21.2	35.7

ᵃ Remaining percentage represents federal expenditure.

ᵇ Alaska and Hawaii omitted.

SOURCE: *Social Security Bulletin: Annual Statistical Supplement, 1959–1961* (Washington: Department of Health, Education and Welfare, 1961), p. 104.

local expenditures to the highest degree possible, although at the same time, they supplement the local effort with relatively heavy state expenditures in order to maintain desired welfare standards.[13]

---

encies to disunity within the state and to tie the various segments of that commonwealth with bonds forged from common interests in sharing the state's resources.

[13] For further discussion of state patterns in the public welfare field, see Richard E. Dawson and James A. Robinson, "The Politics of Welfare," in Jacob and Vines, *op. cit.*, Chapter 10.

State Aid and Local Action

It has frequently been implied that state aid has been the central factor in determining the extent of local action to provide needed government services. In one major sense it has been central. Without state, state-federal, or federal financial assistance, local government activities would remain minimal. Apparently, this has always been true in this country. With the exception of the most basic governmental functions—police and the administration of justice, fire protection, minimal maintenance of streets or roads—where local residents have accepted the burdens of taxation for their support, local governments have been dependent upon outside resources. Even local schools have been subject to this rule in all but a few states, primarily those of New England or those molded by Yankees in the New England pattern, where education was considered an equally basic governmental function very early.

As the activities of local government have expanded beyond the basics, the civil community has become increasingly dependent upon outside aid. In this sense, then, state aid has been a central factor in stimulating the expansion of local government, particularly since most outside aid is state aid and even the federal share is, with a few exceptions, so carefully channeled through the states as to be indistinguishable locally from state-originated funds. The issue is more complex, however. Even when the stimulus for innovation comes from the community leadership, community action is often directed first toward acquiring outside funds to provide the wherewithal for local action. And when the impetus for local government action is then provided by the state (or federal) funds, who is to be considered the stimulator or innovator?

One thing that can be said is that the level of state receptivity to such requests will be of considerable importance. Availability of resources is one common denominator here. New York is likely to be more receptive to spending proposals than Alabama would be, simply because the former has more money to spend. But that is by no means the end of the matter. Cultural factors are of no little importance in determining willingness to spend. Some states are generally more willing to put forth effort for public purposes than are others. All states are more or less receptive to particular proposals for local innovations that coincide with their own policy preferences. Minnesota, for example, is likely to be highly receptive to local innovation in the conservation field and not very receptive to similar innovation in the field of urban mass transit. Colorado is less concerned with promoting conservation programs since the federal government has been so active in that regard within its limits, but is quite receptive to urban-planning activities because of its greatly burgeoning metropolitan population. Pennsylvania, on the other hand, is likely to support (or refuse to support) innovation in both areas equally.

In the last analysis, the extent to which any specific civil community can capitalize on the opportunities available to it within its state and national civil societies depends on the character and constitution of its political system and the individual local governments embodied within it. Though both systems give every civil community and its local governments a multiplicity of "cracks" (both in the sense of blows against the state and federal governments generated locally, and of fissures within the state and federal political systems through which the locally generated blows can penetrate) to use to bend any given program in the direction desired locally, it is the responsibility of the individual civil community to make use of those cracks. If local initiative is not present, the opportunities will remain unrealized.

CHAPTER EIGHT

The Maintenance and Sustenance of the Partnership

Factors Maintaining the System

The system of state-federal relations which has passed in review in the foregoing pages is not the neat system often pictured in the textbooks. If that neat system of separate governments performing separate functions in something akin to isolation is used as the model of what federalism should be to enable the states to maintain their integrity as political systems, then the states are in great difficulty indeed. If, however, the states have found ways to function as integral political systems—civil societies, if you will —within the somewhat chaotic system of intergovernmental sharing that exists, then they are, as the saying goes, in a different ball game.

In the previous chapters we have tried to show that the states are indeed in a different ball game and as players in that game are not doing badly at all. Viewed from the perspective of that ball game, the strength and vitality of the states—and the strength and vitality of the American system as a whole—must be assessed by different standards from those commonly used.

In the first place, the states exist. This point is no less significant for its simplicity. The fact that the states survive as going concerns (as distinct from sets of historical boundaries used for the administration of centrally directed programs) after thirty-five years of depression, global war, and then cold war, which have all functioned to reduce the domestic freedom necessary to preserve noncentralized government, is in itself testimony to their vitality as political institutions. And, as was indicated in Chapter One, anyone who doubts the states' existence as going concerns need only look at the stand the few really recalcitrant states have been able to maintain on the segregation issue. Better, if less dramatic, examples of the states' existence as vital and contributing elements in the nation's political system have also been cited. Every day, in many ways, the states are actively contributing to the achievement of American goals and to the continuing efforts to define those goals.

Consequently, it is a mistake to think that national adoption of goals shared by an overwhelming majority of the states is simply centralization. To believe that is to deny the operation of the dynamics of history within a federal system. Any assessment of the states' position in the federal union must be made against a background of continuous social change. It is no more reasonable to assume that the states have lost power vis-à-vis the federal government since 1789 because they can no longer maintain established churches than it is to believe that white men are no longer as free as they were in that year because they can no longer own slaves. An apparent loss of freedom in one sphere may be more than made up by gains in another. Massachusetts exercises more power over its economy today than its governors ever hoped to exercise over its churches five generations ago. National values change by popular consensus and *all* governments must adapt themselves to those changes. The success of the states is that they have been able to adapt themselves well.

Part of the states' adaptation has been manifested in their efforts to improve their institutional capabilities to handle the new tasks they have assumed. In the twentieth century, there has been an extensive and continuing reorganization of state governments leading to increased executive responsibility, greater central budgetary control, and growing expertise of state personnel (whose numbers are also increasing). While the progress of the states in these areas has varied considerably, in general the larger states with the most need for such organizational improvements have been the ones to adopt them. This subject has been explored elsewhere and need not be treated here.[1]

There has also been a great and continuing increase in the states' supervision of the functions carried out in their local subdivisions. The states' role in this respect has grown as fast as or faster than that of the federal government and is often exercised more stringently, a possibility enhanced by the constitutionally unitary character of the states. The states' supervision has been increased through the provision of technical aid to their localities, through financial grants, and through control of the power to raise (or authorize the raising of) revenue for all subdivisions.

In all this, though, there remains one major unsolved problem, whose importance cannot be overemphasized: that of the metropolitan areas. By and large, the states have been unwilling or unable to do enough to meet metropolitan problems, particularly governmental ones. Here, too, some states have better records than others but none have been able to deal with metropolitan problems comprehensively and thoroughly. It is becoming increasingly clear that—whatever their successes in the past—the

Table 21. State Revenues from Own Sources, 1948–1961 (Selected Years; in millions)

1948	$10,086
1950	11,480
1952	14,330
1954	15,951
1956	18,903
1958	21,427
1960	26,093
1961	27,821

SOURCE: Tax Foundation, *Facts and Figures on Government Finance, 1962–1963*, 12th ed. (Englewood Cliffs, N.J.: Prentice-Hall, 1963).

[1] See, for example, Duane Lockard, *The Politics of State and Local Government* (New York: Macmillan, 1963), Chapters 12 and 13, and Coleman B. Ransone, Jr., *The Office of Governor in the United States* (University, Ala.: University of Alabama Press, 1956).

Table 22. State Expenditures from Own Revenues, 1948–1962 [a] (Selected Fiscal Years)

YEAR	TOTAL EXPEND-ITURES (IN MILLIONS)	PER CAP-ITA	PER CENT OF TOTAL GOVT. EXPENDITURE	TOTAL PAYMENTS TO LOCAL GOVTS. (IN MILLIONS) [b]
1948	$ 9,531	$ 66	17.3	$ 3,283
1950	12,774	86	18.2	4,217
1952	13,330	87	13.4	5,044
1954	15,803	100	14.2	5,679
1956	18,379	112	15.9	6,538
1958	23,338	137	17.3	8,089
1960	24,881	140	16.4	9,443
1962	29,200	160	16.7	10,114 (1961)

[a] Excludes federal transfers.

[b] Includes federal transfers where passed on to local governments.

SOURCE: Tax Foundation, Facts and Figures on Government Finance, 1962–1963, 12th ed. (Englewood Cliffs, N.J.: Prentice-Hall, 1963).

future role of the states will be determined by their ability to come to grips with those problems.

A fourth factor that adds to the strength and vitality of the states is the manner in which state revenues and expenditures have been expanding since the end of World War II. Some relevant figures are presented in Tables 21 and 22. These figures include only funds raised by the states from their own sources. The addition of federal transfers would substantially increase the total amounts spent by the states. What these gross figures do not reveal is the growth of state expenditures in areas unaffected by federal grants as well as in areas where state matching funds are required to obtain federal aid. Table 23 compares the growth of the federal government and the states in the four categories of revenues, expenditures, debt, and employment, plus the growth in intergovernmental payments over two periods, 1939–40 to 1949–50 and 1949–50 to 1961–62. In all but one category, the states with their local subdivisions have had a greater rate of growth since 1949–50.

Perhaps an even better indication of the strength of the

Factors Maintaining the System

Table 23. Relative Growth of the Federal and State Governments, 1939–1962

	PERCENTAGE INCREASES	
LEVEL AND ITEM	1939–40 TO 1949–50	1949–50 TO 1961–62
Revenues		
Federal (Budget Receipts)	608	123
State-Local (Total Revenue)	118	123
Expenditures		
Federal (Budget Expenditures)	336	125
Domestic-Civilian Expenditures	191	54
State-Local (Total Expenditures)	148	138
Debt		
Federal	499	15
State-Local	19	213
Employment		
Federal-Civilian	81	21
State-Level	24	59
Intergovernmental Payments		
Federal-State/Local	163	184
State-Local	155	140

SOURCE: Tax Foundation, *Facts and Figures on Government Finance, 1962–1963,* 12th ed. (Englewood Cliffs, N.J.: Prentice-Hall, 1963).

states is their role in the national economy. In 1949, the gross national product was $258,054 billion of which government purchases of goods and services accounted for $40,159 billion— $22,241 billion by the federal government and $17,918 billion by the states and their local subdivisions. By 1961, the GNP had grown to $518,725 billion and government purchase of goods and services had grown to $107,430 billion. The federal share of the latter figure was $56,997 billion while the state-local share had risen to $50,433 billion.[2]

Still a fifth factor is the continuing role of the states as primary managers of great programs and as important innovators in the governmental realm. Both management and innovation in

[2] Figures from *Facts and Figures on Government Finance, 1962–1963,* 12th ed. (Englewood Cliffs, N.J.: Prentice-Hall, 1963).

education, for example, continue to be primary state responsibilities in which outside aid is used to support locally initiated ideas. The states' role in higher education is greater than that of most nations. California alone spends over $400 million of state funds annually for over 650,000 full-time students enrolled in its complex of colleges and universities—far more students than in France, Great Britain, West Germany, and the Benelux countries combined. Eight states support higher education systems with much larger enrollments than that of the United Kingdom. In 1965, responding to widespread pressures for formulating nationwide educational standards, the states inaugurated an interstate compact on education. This compact establishes an advisory commission to develop educational policies representing all fifty states plus the federal government, thus obviating the necessity for federal intervention in substantive matters of national educational concern.

Even in areas of apparent state deficiencies, many states pursue innovative policies. Much publicity has been generated in recent years that reflects upon police procedures in certain states; yet effective actions to eliminate the death penalty have been confined to the state level. The states have also been active in developing means for releasing persons accused of crimes on their own recognizance when they cannot afford to post bail, thus reducing the imprisonment of people not yet convicted of criminal activity.[3]

Because the states are political systems able to direct the utilization of the resources sent their way, federal grants have served as a stimulus to the development of state capabilities and, hence, have helped enhance their strength and vitality. Federal grants have helped the states in a positive way by broadening the programs they can offer their citizens and strengthening state administration of those programs. Conversely, the grants have prevented centralization of those programs and have given the

---

[3] For an annual review of state activities that points up their role in the federal system, see the article "States, U.S." in the *Britannica Book of the Year* (Chicago: Encyclopedia Britannica, Inc., published annually).

states the ability to maintain their position despite the centralizing tendencies of the times.

For this reason, and because the concerns of American politics are universal ones, there is relatively little basic conflict between the federal government and the states or even between their respective interests. Most of the conflicts connected with federal-state relations are of two kinds: (1) conflicts between interests that use the federal versus state argument as a means to legitimize their demands or (2) low-level conflicts over the best way to handle specific cooperative activities. There are cases, of course, when interests representing real differences are able to align themselves with different levels of government to create serious federal-state conflict. The civil rights question in its southern manifestation is today's example of that kind of situation.

Finally, the noncentralized character of American politics has served to strengthen the states. Noncentralization makes possible intergovernment cooperation without the concomitant weakening of the smaller partners by giving those partners significant ways in which to preserve their integrity. This is because a noncentralized system functions to a great extent through bargaining and negotiation. Since its components are relatively equal in their freedom to act, it can utilize only a few of the hierarchical powers available in centralized systems. In essence, its general government can only use those powers set forth in the fundamental compact between the partners as necessary to the maintenance of the system as a whole. Stated baldly, congressional authorization of new federal programs is frequently no more than a license allowing federal authorities to begin negotiations with the states and localities.

American federalism is immediately sustained by the party system which has emerged as a product of its principles and now serves to maintain those principles. In a noncentralized political system, the parties have been almost a caricature of the principles of noncentralization. The political parties, starting from their bases in the fifty states, represent the bargaining system in its most extreme form. With some 514,000 elective local officials and 12,000 to 15,000 more elected state officials in the United States, serving nearly 100,000 different governments, there is literally one elective office for every 100 families in the country. Even after the nonpartisan offices are eliminated, most of these positions are filled by people who are not beholden to any party organization and are thus free to relate to the party system as they choose.

In many cases, these offices are occupied by people with little political ambition who have been prevailed upon to fill vacuums. They, of course, can hardly be coerced from above since it is not to their advantage to exchange their attachments to their constituencies for distant control. If the officeholders are interested in office, their interest is primarily directed to appealing to their constituencies or, at the very most, in appealing to the next largest constituency to which they aspire. Those constituencies are—excepting only the presidency and vice-presidency—either states or established by the states. If the officeholders or others active in politics are interested in substantive rewards for political activity, the states and localities have more of these to distribute, ranging from jobs to contracts to "fixing" traffic tickets. In all three cases, only a bargaining relationship can tie the officeholders to larger political bodies and the state parties have the best means to turn the bargaining system to their advantage.[4]

Public Response: The Sustenance of the System

This system of state-federal cooperation appears to be maintaining its hold on the American people despite its many critics to the right and left and the amazing ignorance of most Americans as to how it works. The system is sustained because it provides most of the competing interests in the United States—even those groups which denounce it as encroaching upon the rights of local self-government and those which attack it for abandoning national

[4] Herbert Kaufman discusses this more fully in *Politics and Policies in State and Local Governments* (Englewood Cliffs, N.J.: Prentice-Hall, 1963), pp. 12–20.

goals in favor of local selfishness—with enough satisfactions to convince them that it works. And it provides those satisfactions because it is amenable to political influence in the deepest sense at every level. Despite the headlines which tend to present one level of government as "the good guys" and the other as "the bad guys" (the choice depends upon one's political outlook), most interests can gain some satisfaction at every level.

Perhaps there was a time when it was possible to generalize casually about specific interests being satisfied by different levels of government, to establish a precarious balance between the federal government, the states, and the localities by virtue of these different sources of satisfaction. There appear to have been grounds to support this view a generation ago. Today it is simply no longer true about any significant interests. Every interest now tries to develop ties with every level of government and will utilize those ties to varying degrees depending upon the specific issue confronting it. This is no doubt a natural concomitant of the growing complexity of the sharing system and the increasing involvement of all levels of government in handling the same programs.

Three generations ago and more, the analyst would probably have thought it strange to think of interests' aligning themselves

Table 24. Appeal to Government by Level in the Pre-Civil War Period

	FOR	AGAINST
Southern slave-holders	Use of federal powers to protect slave owners in territories. Federal fugitive slave laws. Rights of states to maintain slavery.	Federal delivery of Abolitionist propaganda. Northern-state personal liberty laws.
Northern anti-slavery forces	Federal prohibition of slavery in territories. Rights of states to protect fugitive slaves.	Federal enforcement of fugitive slave laws. Rights of states to maintain slavery.

with specific levels of government. During the nineteenth century when cooperative federalism revolved around land grants and joint stock companies, all levels of government were involved in the same programs. Sharing then, like sharing now, prevented a serious alignment of interests by government level. Despite all myths to the contrary, both northern abolitionists and southern slave owners appealed to all three levels of government at various times to support their respective positions (Table 24).

It was only with the rise of labor-management antagonisms that the notion of separate appeals came to the fore. Even then, at the beginning both interests found similar kinds of support or antagonism at both the federal and state levels. Usually the industrialists held the dominant position at both levels and were able to utilize both governments to limit the abilities of the workers to organize and to interfere with their right to strike. True, there were important exceptions to this rule. In some states, Populist-influenced governments were inclined to take the side of labor, and from time to time national administrations adopted a hands-off policy. No continuing differences developed, however, until the 1930's when the federal government under Democratic control adopted an open prolabor position and the industrialists fell back on the states. Since the labor-management question bulked so large among the public concerns of the thirties, the consequences that flowed from it were raised by political analysts from the level of the specific issue which spawned them to become the basis for sweeping generalizations about the political system. Hence the notion of separate appeals, valid in this issue, was raised to the level of generalization.

At least since the mid-1950's, labor and management have once again made their appeals on the basis of an immediate multiplicity of specific interests rather than in reference to one overriding concern. This meant the end of division by level. Management, while still happier with its relationships at the state level, found a sympathetic administration in Washington under President Eisenhower, and organized labor, though still strongly in favor of active federal intervention in the nation's domestic affairs, discovered that it neglected the states at its own peril. The

Public Response: The Sustenance of the System

Taft-Hartley Act opened the doors to discretionary action on the part of the states in such aspects of labor regulation as compulsory union membership, and twenty of the less industrialized southern and western states soon enacted right-to-work laws prohibiting the closed shop in its several forms.[5] The governments of the northern and western industrialized states were open to labor influence, and Democratic governors elected through the efforts of the unions took office in state capitols from coast to coast. In those states, labor stopped right-to-work-law movements cold by stepping into a newly active role.

The necessity for organizing influence at the state level was nowhere more clearly revealed to organized labor than in the newly industrialized or semi-industrialized states. In Colorado, in Oklahoma, and in Washington, right-to-work legislation actually reached the voting stage and was stopped only by labor efforts to reach each state's public.

Conversely, business interests active in the states to restrict the power of organized labor were equally active in Washington for other reasons. Airlines and shipping companies sought to gain or maintain federal subsidies. Small businesses sought federal technical assistance, loans at special interest rates, and aid in obtaining defense contracts. A whole new set of big business interests developed as a consequence of federal expenditures for defense, all with close and continuing relationships at the federal level.

Nor is alignment by level as significant as it is often made out to be in the civil rights issue that remains the greatest point of state federal conflict in the United States today. It is often, and rightly, said that the Negroes are especially oriented toward Washington from whence comes their help. The ability of the southern states to obstruct federal action to insure the civil rights of all Americans makes this so. That should not obscure the fact that the Negroes and other minority groups were able to gain

[5] In 1965, Indiana repealed its right-to-work law as a result of the successful efforts of a Democratic-labor coalition to elect a majority in the state legislature in what can be considered a clear indication of the meaning of this paragraph.

legislative assistance to prevent discrimination in more than thirty states before Congress was able to respond to similar requests. Certainly it would be inaccurate to describe the federal government as more favorable to the cause of Negro rights than states like New York, Minnesota, Michigan, or Colorado. Indeed, while some states have given the public a sense that states' rights must be synonymous with racial discrimination, nearly three times as many states have utilized those same rights to combat discrimination as fully as the federal Congress. And most of them were able to act even during the years when Congress was held back by the Dixiecrat-Republican coalition. So it is with many other issues as well.

"Squeak Points" in the System

There are, indeed, certain clear points of tension within the present federal-state partnership that work to weaken the states as political systems. At various times, the spokesmen for the states have summarized the problems facing them as a result of those points of tension. Some of their criticisms may be outlined here.

Modern governments maintain control over their variegated activities through the budgetary process. Thus maintenance of a centrally managed budget is an essential prerequisite for a smoothly running political system. Some of the greatest difficulties faced by the state as political systems stem from the lack of harmonization of federal and state budgetary processes. Because federal appropriations are voted on an annual basis and many states operate on biennial budgets, the central governing agencies of the states have great difficulty in planning their programs involving federal aid and in coordinating them with other state functions. They do not know how much federal aid will be available and in what form until Congress has acted. Moreover, the large number of separate federal aid programs introduces a chaotic note in state budgeting, tending to impair the maintenance of an executive budget. Some kind of coordinated activity at the federal level would enable the states to participate in federal aid programs while maintaining their overall governmental programs on a more integrated basis.

In the smaller states at least, federal aid programs tend to skew state appropriations in favor of those activities that have federal support. When a state can, in effect, obtain two dollars by the expenditure of one, such programs obviously will be given some preferential treatment. This problem has diminished somewhat because of the greater amount of money available in most states, giving them added flexibility. Also, the proliferation of small federal grant programs in addition to the large ones that are universally utilized encourages more states to pick and choose. Even so, the problem remains.

The allocation of most categorical grants for narrowly specific purposes denies the states the flexibility they need to handle their own particular variations of nationwide problems. In the course of their negotiations with their federal counterparts concerning the use of categorical grants, state officials are often able to gain more flexibility than the law allows on its face, but the barriers of legal "earmarking" remain and are particularly harmful to those states actively endeavoring to develop sound comprehensive programs based on local needs. Block grants in major fields, whereby the states would receive funds designated for very general purposes and would be able to allocate them for specific activities according to their special needs, have been suggested as a means to overcome this problem.

Moreover, the proliferation of federal agencies to handle new federal aid programs in recent years increases the danger of aggressive federal efforts to promote nationwide uniformity even in peripheral fields, reducing the area of state discretion and interfering with legitimate local decision-making without stopping to differentiate between programs that clearly require nationwide equalization and those that can legitimately reflect local diversity, maintenance of which is equally in the national interest.

Aside from the budgetary problem, state integrity is challenged by the number of federal administrative requirements that sometimes proliferate excessively in an effort to insure state compliance with the terms of the law. Some of the worst features of bureaucratic control are manifest in a number of the federal aid programs. Some administrative forms are so complex that they make administration unnecessarily unwieldy. Often great amounts of irrelevant information are required. States frequently experience troublesome delays in obtaining needed decisions from regional and national offices. Sometimes authority to act in behalf of federal agencies is not clearly spelled out; at times federal agents will be too indecisive, at other times too arbitrary. While the state can usually find ways to cut through these problems, by hook or crook, they are, at the very best, nuisances that delay joint projects, and, at the worst, unwarranted federal interference into processes legitimately the province of the states.

State integrity is further challenged by certain kinds of direct federal-local relationships. Federal programs that deal directly with the cities tend to unsettle the states' relationships with their subdivisions. Even the most liberal state leaders would argue that direct federal-local arrangements should exist only when the state provides no suitable mechanism for the federal aid programs. Recently this problem has been magnified with the introduction of direct federal grants to local community agencies that, while serving public purposes, are not governmental and are not accountable to the state or local publics. Though most of the new programs inaugurated by Congress since 1961 fall within the overall framework of cooperative federalism, the tendency to bypass the states has markedly increased. Of the sixteen separate grant programs enacted into law by the Second Session of the Eighty-eighth Congress (the first to come under the influence of President Johnson), only seven were definitely channeled through the states. Six others could be channeled through the states or transmitted directly to local and private agencies and three were explicitly designed to go directly to the latter. More important, however, from two-fifths to one-half of the total new expenditures authorized for those programs, including some $340 million for general community action programs under the Economic Opportunity Act of 1964, were to go to specific agencies in such a way as to maintain opportunities for state or local coordination of the various grants made within their areas of jurisdiction.

The historical record shows that direct federal-local and federal-private programs in the past, unlike those involving the states, were often quite wasteful and, at least in the case of federal aid to nongovernmental agencies, were often tainted with scandal on a large scale. There is, of course, no guarantee that history will be repeated today, but there appear to be substantial grounds for believing that the channeling of federal aid through the states has a salutary effect on the responsible use of that aid, even beyond the important consideration that the health of the federal system is enhanced when the states retain the right to integrate all governmental functions within their jurisdiction or the jurisdiction of their subdivisions into an overall policy framework.

A description of the "squeak points" in the state-federal relationship is not meant to suggest there is much evidence that the states are basically dissatisfied with federal programs. One of the revealing aspects of the many intergovernmental studies conducted in the past decade is the lack of criticism on the part of state administrative officials concerning ongoing federal programs. State administrators almost uniformly approve the programs and voice apprehension over any prospective diminution in them. Such criticism as there is tends to come from the state legislators who respond to more traditional "anticentralization" ideas.[6]

Finally, the proliferation of new federal aid programs planned in Washington without prior consultation with those who are responsible for general government in the states—the governors and legislatures—raises other problems of breaking down the cohesiveness of the states as civil societies, preventing, as it does, the development of new programs along lines that harmonize with the partnership system and limiting the possibilities of advance planning for new programs in the states. The

[6] The hearings of the (Fountain) Subcommittee on Intergovernmental Relations of the House Committee on Government Operations provide the best and clearest source of data to this effect.

states, on the other hand, add to their difficulties by failing to take the steps necessary to assimilate outside aids within an over-all program. Lack of adequate staff services for governors and legislatures denies them the opportunity to exercise general supervision over cooperative programs or to plan for the proper integration of federal aid.

If anything, the spokesmen for the states have been calling for more federal aid in one form or another. Governors as well as mayors have been journeying regularly to Washington to testify on behalf of federal aid programs or in search of federal aid for specific projects in their states, usually without discrimination as to the agency that will be formally responsible for implementation of the projects. Regardless of the public pronouncements some of them make from time to time denouncing "federal encroachments," none have shown serious interest in the efforts to devolve shared functions back to the states.[7] When he was governor of Minnesota, Orville Freeman put the matter succinctly in testimony before the Joint Federal-State Action Committee, which had been created to find ways to return functions to the states:

I believe the plight of our states demands an expansion and extension of federal support, not curtailment or abandonment of programs of assistance. Historically, federal grants-in-aid have certainly increased, not decreased, the scope of state activities. The best way to ensure strengthened vitality at both national and state levels of the federal system is to continue and to enlarge the cooperation and collaboration between them. Instead of agitating for the discontinuance of certain federal-state programs, we should examine prospects for more of them.

Governor Freeman's remarks were made in 1958, after a period of relative federal retrenchment. In the mid-1960's, after several years of federal activism and the inauguration of billions of dollars of new federal programs, some of which will strengthen

---

[7] For a thorough discussion of these efforts to devolve functions and the reasons for their failure, see Morton Grodzins, "Why Decentralization by Order Won't Work," in Edward C. Banfield, ed., *Urban Government* (New York: Free Press of Glencoe, 1961), pp. 122–131.

the states and others of which may not, this sentiment may have diminished substantially.

Another point of Freeman's has attracted renewed interest in the states, however:

> The time has come for courageously asking whether the federal government should not share with the states a portion of its plentiful tax sources. It may be wiser in the long run, instead of cutting the federal income tax by several billions as is currently proposed, to retain the present rates and bring much-needed federal relief to the states, thereby making unnecessary tax increases at the state level . . . One measure might be that the Congress return to the states a portion—perhaps 5 percent—of the federal corporate and individual income tax.[8]

This proposal has since been publicly suggested as the "Heller Plan," named after the former chairman of the President's Council of Economic Advisors who had previously served Freeman as an economic adviser in Minnesota. At this writing, it and similar plans are being discussed among the range of groups, agencies, and institutions concerned with state-federal relations.

An observer sympathetic to the federal system and interested in the maintenance of the states might see several other problems threatening them as political systems. One is their seeming inability to gain public attention except in times of crisis or when they are having problems that do not reflect creditably upon them. This is partly a problem of the mass media which has come to focus on Washington, not only because so much news is made there, but because it is more convenient. It is partly a problem of public unconcern which affects Americans' understanding of their political system generally.

This tendency to ignore the states is no doubt one reflection of America's dramatic involvement in world affairs. Nothing short of a racial clash in Little Rock or Selma is likely to rival the drama of Berlin or Viet Nam. And in the last generation there have been a succession of Berlins and Viet Nams. The threat to the states is not simply a question of dramatics or imagery. It may

[8] Proceedings of the 1958 Governors' Conference, p. 30 ff.

be that, as the United States becomes more deeply entangled with the world, it is less likely to have time or energy to exercise the self-restraint needed to maintain a domestic system of non-centralization that requires a certain amount of time-consuming bargaining and negotiation to make it function. The full extent of this problem is not known but its consequences are far-reaching.

There is already a certain amount of sentiment in favor of "simpler" solutions to domestic problems so that the nation may get on with its foreign concerns. This sentiment is usually espoused by those who seek immediate and drastic solutions to some specific domestic problem, solutions that are not likely to be adopted in pure form under the present system. There has always been a contradiction between federal democracy—popular government based on a covenant relationship among the governors and the governed that requires due consideration for the individual rights of all parties to the compact—and Jacobin democracy, or rule by simple majority in the name of the general will.[9] The former offers a path to free decision-making that has roadblocks at crucial points to check those trodding it and force them to balance their desires with those of others whose interests are at stake, while the latter seeks the most direct path for the majority to follow, one with the roadblocks designed to protect minorities removed. Federal democracy demands self-restraint, particularly on the part of those who hold power. It is impatience with this self-restraint that breeds Jacobins in every generation. In the course of American history, the Jacobins have occasionally won victories but in every case have ultimately been restrained by the great good sense of the American people. In most of the world, however, Jacobinism in its variant forms has become synonymous

[9] The Jacobin approach can be found in many public statements issued by popular students of American government today. One of the best presentations is James MacGregor Burns, *The Deadlock of Democracy* (New York: Prentice-Hall, 1963). The classic statement of the federal approach is *The Federalist*. More recent statements include Martin Diamond, "Democracy and *The Federalist*: A Reconsideration of the Framers' Intent," *American Political Science Review*, XIII (March, 1959). Walter Lippmann contrasts the two approaches in *The Public Philosophy* (Boston: Atlantic-Little, Brown, 1955).

with democracy. As the United States comes to share ideas with the larger world, only clear understanding and articulation of its unique federal principles will make it possible to perpetuate them in the public mind and in the American system of government itself.

Virtues of the System

In the last analysis, the states remain viable entities in a federal system that has every tendency toward centralization present in all strong governments. They remain viable because they exist as civil societies with political systems of their own. They maintain that existence because the American political tradition and the Constitution embodying it give the states an important place in the overall fabric of American civil society. The tradition and the Constitution remain viable because neither Capitol Hill nor the fifty state houses have alone been able to serve all the variegated interests on the American scene that compete equally well without working in partnership.

The states remain vital political systems for larger reasons as well as immediate ones, reasons that are often passed over unnoticed in the public's concern with day-to-day problems of government. These larger reasons are not new; though they have changed in certain details, they remain essentially the same as in the early days of the Union.[10]

The states remain important in a continental nation as reflectors of sectional and regional differences that are enhanced by the growing social and economic complexity of every part of the country, even as the older cultural differences may be diminished by modern communications. They remain important as experimenters and innovators over a wider range of fields than ever before, simply because government at every level in the United States has been expanding. The role of the states as recruiters of

[10] The following summary is meant to be suggestive rather than exhaustive. A full-scale discussion of the problem remains to be undertaken, but for further reading on the subject, see George C. S. Benson, "Values of Decentralized Government—1961," in *Essays in Federalism* (Claremont, Calif.: Institute for Studies in Federalism, 1961).

political participants and trainers of political leaders has in no way been diminished, particularly since the number of political offices of every kind seems to be increasing at least in proportion to population growth.

In at least two ways, traditional roles of the states have been enhanced by recent trends. They have become even more active promoters and administrators of public services than ever before. In part, this is simply because governments are doing more than they had in the past, but it is also because they provide ways to increase governmental activity while maintaining noncentralized government. By handling important programs at a level that can be reached by many people, they contribute to the maintenance of a traditional interest of democratic politics, namely, the maximization of local control over the political and administrative decision-makers whose actions affect the lives of every citizen in ever-increasing ways.

As the population of the nation increases, the states become increasingly able to manage major governmental activities with the competence and expertise demanded by the metropolitan-technological frontier. At the same time, the federal government becomes further removed from popular pressures simply by virtue of the increased size of the population it must serve. The states may well be on their way to becoming the most "manageable" civil societies in the nation. Their size and scale remain comprehensible to people even as they are enabled to do more things better.

In sum, the virtue of the federal system lies in its ability to develop and maintain mechanisms vital to the perpetuation of the unique combination of governmental strength, political flexibility, and individual liberty, which has been the central concern of American politics. The American people are known to appreciate their political tradition and the Constitution. Most important, they seem to appreciate the partnership, too, in some unreasoned way, and have learned to use all its elements to reasonably satisfy their claims on government.

For Further Reading

Recent Books

ADRIAN, CHARLES R., *Governing Our Fifty States and Their Communities* (New York: McGraw-Hill, 1963).

A good introduction to the study of the states as political systems which emphasizes the basics of state and local government.

ANDERSON, WILLIAM, *The Nation and the States, Rivals or Partners?* (Minneapolis: University of Minnesota Press, 1955).

Anderson's minority report for the (Kestnbaum) Commission on Intergovernmental Relations setting forth his views on the legitimacy and strength of cooperative Federalism.

ANDERSON, WILLIAM, and EDWARD WEIDNER, *Intergovernmental Relations in Minnesota* (Minneapolis: University of Minnesota Press, 1948–1962), 10 vols.

A series of individually authored reports studying various aspects of the federal-state-local relationship in Minnesota, including fiscal affairs, functional aspects of government, specific programs, and specific local problems.

ELAZAR, DANIEL J., *The American Partnership* (Chicago: University of Chicago Press, 1962).

A study of the evolution of cooperative federalism before 1913, stressing federal-state sharing of program administration and financing from the early days of the Republic, and the politics behind the evolution of sharing.

GOLDWIN, ROBERT, ed., *A Nation of States* (Chicago: Rand McNally, 1962).

A collection of articles on various aspects of American federalism that provides both a view of the system as it operates and a review of the arguments about how it should operate.

GRAVES, W. BROOKE, *American Intergovernmental Relations* (New York: Scribner's, 1964).

A comprehensive overview of the federal system by one who

has studied the workings of the system for over a generation.

GRODZINS, MORTON, *The American System: A New View of Government in the United States,* ed. Daniel J. Elazar (Chicago: Rand McNally, 1966).

The most important recent study of the American federal system by the leading contemporary student of American federalism, describing the workings of the federal system from the cooperative point of view and setting forth certain basic hypotheses to use in understanding the system.

KAUFMAN, HERBERT, *Politics and Policies in State and Local Governments* (Englewood Cliffs, N.J.: Prentice-Hall, 1963).

A very perceptive and well-written introduction to state and local politics with particular emphasis on the states as parts of the federal system and containing useful tabular data.

KEY, V. O., JR., *American State Politics: An Introduction* (New York: Knopf, 1956).

The first of the recent studies of state politics which set down many of the fundamental hypotheses and raised many of the important questions being studied today.

LOCKARD, DUANE, *The Politics of State and Local Government* (New York: Macmillan, 1963).

One of the best of the recent texts on state and local government.

MAC MAHAN, ARTHUR W., ed., *Federalism: Mature and Emergent* (New York: Macmillan, 1955).

An excellent collection of articles on various aspects of federalism by leading specialists. Primarily devoted to analyzing American federalism, it also deals with federal experiences in other countries and prospects for the use of federalism to unify Europe and the developing nations.

REYNOLDS, HARRY W., JR., ed., *Intergovernmental Relations in the United States* (*The Annals of the American Academy of Political and Social Science,* CCCLIX, May 1965).

A collection of articles on current trends and practices in American federalism that serves to bring the recent book-length studies up to date.

For Further Reading

Government Reports

Library of Congress, Legislative Reference Service, *Catalog of Federal Aids to State and Local Governments* (April 1964) and *Supplement* (January 1965), U.S. Senate Committee on Government Operations, Subcommittee on Intergovernmental Relations.
An annotated catalog of all formal federal aids available to state and local governments containing descriptions of each program and a listing of the federal agencies responsible for administering each.

REPORT OF THE COMMISSION ON INTERGOVERNMENTAL RELATIONS, 1955, 16 vols.
This is the report of the well-known Kestnbaum Commission, appointed by President Eisenhower to undertake the first complete study of American federalism by an official body. Its report and the accompanying task force studies form the basis for much of the contemporary research in the field of American federalism.

REPORTS OF THE ADVISORY COMMISSION ON INTERGOVERNMENTAL RELATIONS.
This is the permanent body created at the end of the Eisenhower Administration to provide a continuing review of federal-state-local relations and to promote action to make the federal system function more smoothly. It includes representatives from all levels of government, has a permanent staff, and issues several reports each year, dealing with many aspects of federal-state-local relations including state-local relations and metropolitan area problems.

REPORTS OF THE JOINT COMMITTEE ON INTERGOVERNMENTAL RELATIONS, 1958 AND 1959.
This was the second Eisenhower-appointed body to study problems of federalism. Its purpose was to determine how to turn functions back to the states and which functions to return. Its two reports are most interesting for their limited recommendations and the discussion explaining why they are so limited.

REPORTS OF THE SUBCOMMITTEE ON INTERGOVERNMENTAL RELA-
TIONS, HOUSE COMMITTEE ON GOVERNMENT OPERATIONS.

This is the Fountain Subcommittee which has been studying
intergovernmental relations since 1956. The published tran-
scripts of its hearings and the reports based on question-
naires sent to those involved in intergovernmental programs
contain important data on the federal system.

REPORTS OF THE SUBCOMMITTEE ON INTERGOVERNMENTAL RELA-
TIONS, SENATE COMMITTEE ON GOVERNMENT OPERATIONS

This is the Muskie Subcommittee which began to function
in 1961. Its work parallels and supplements that of the Fountain Subcommittee.

U.S. DEPARTMENT OF COMMERCE, BUREAU OF THE CENSUS, *Census of Governments, 1962.*

This multivolume report is an invaluable compendium of
data on governments at all levels in the United States and
is particularly important in the study of state and local government. Similar censuses were taken in 1941, 1952, 1957.

Periodicals and Serial Publications

The Book of the States, published biennially by the Council of
State Governments with a supplement in the off-years.

A compendium of data on state officials and administration,
with summaries of important state actions in various fields.

Britannica Book of the Year (Chicago: Encyclopedia Britannica,
Inc., published annually).

The article "States, U.S." summarizes principal state activities
with particular reference to the role of the states in the
federal system.

State Government, published quarterly by the Council of State
Governments.

Contains articles on state government and its problems and
intergovernmental relations.

State Government News, published monthly by the Council of
State Governments.

Provides immediate data on current actions of the states and
federal activities affecting the states.

INDEX

Index

Index

Louisiana (*cont.*)
  state-local relations in, 181-182, 185, 187, 190, 192
Lubell, Samuel, 100n, 104n

McKean, Eugene C., 75n
Maine, 16, 18, 133: political culture of, 96, 108, 110, 113, 122; state-local relations in, 181, 182, 185, 187, 190, 192
Maryland, 9, 16, 18, 133: political cultures of, 96, 101, 108, 110, 122; state-local relations in, 181, 182, 187, 190, 193
Massachusetts, 73, 82, 136, 198: internal unity of, 16, 18, 20, 147n; metropolitan center in, 133, 177, 179; political cultures of, 96, 103, 108, 110, 113, 118-119, 122; state-local relations in, 181, 182, 187, 190, 193
Matthews, Donald R., 126n
megalopolis, 114, 131
merit system, 28, 31, 92: and patronage systems, 37, 89; state standards of, 82
Merton, Robert K., 25n
metropolitan areas: as civil societies, 176-179; and the frontier process, 98-99; problems of, 16, 17, 21, 133, 162, 199-200; and sectionalism, 131-135; and state conflict, 119, 182-186; *see also* cities
metropolitan-technological frontier, 98-99, 100n, 104, 113, 131-139
Michigan, 75, 136, 177, 208: internal unity of, 16, 18, 21; political cultures of, 96, 100, 108, 110, 122; state-local relations in, 181, 182, 187, 190, 193
Middle West, the, 21, 100, 101, 105, 113
migrations, and political culture, 95, 97-105
Milbrath, Lester W., 120n, 121n
militia, state, 41, 45, 83-84
Minnesota, 61, 71n, 82, 83, 133, 208: constitution of, 45; internal unity of, 16, 18, 19, 20; political culture of, 96, 100, 108, 110, 119, 122; state-local relations in, 164, 181, 182, 187, 190, 193, 194

Mississippi, 8, 9, 16, 18, 83: political culture of, 96, 102, 108, 110, 122; state-local relations in, 181, 182, 184, 187, 190, 192; voting in, 12, 155, 155n
Missouri, 9, 16, 18, 135: political cultures of, 96, 101, 102, 108, 110, 122; state-local relations in, 179n, 181, 182, 184, 185, 186, 187, 190
Montana, 16, 18: political cultures of, 96, 100, 103, 108, 110, 122; state-local relations in, 181, 182, 187, 190, 193
moralistic (M) political culture, 86, 89-92, 105-106, 117-126, 135-136, 156: state distribution of, 96, 100-111; the term, 86, 109
Mort, Paul, 190n
Mowry, George E., 105n
municipal corporations, 164-166
Murphy, Walter F., 13n

National Association of County Officials, 160
National Conference of Commissioners on Uniform State Laws, 159, 161
National Education Association, 151, 190, 191
National Guard, 29, 83
National Municipal League, 160
Nebraska, 16, 18, 21: political cultures of, 96, 101-102, 108, 110, 122; state-local relations in, 133, 181, 182, 187, 190, 193
Negroes: in Mississippi politics, 155n; population, 135-136; and Washington, D.C., 207-208; *see also* civil rights
Nevada, 16, 18, 133: political culture of, 96, 102, 108, 110, 122; state-local relations in, 181, 183, 187, 190, 193
New England, 74, 99-100, 110, 136: intrastate unity in, 19, 20; and sectionalism, 94-95, 112-113, 116; state-local relations in, 184-188, 190, 194
New Hampshire, 16, 18, 133: political cultures of, 96, 108, 110, 113, 122; state-local relations in, 181, 183, 185, 187, 190, 193

Index

Index